A Keyboard Approach

HARMONIC FOUNDATION FOR JAZZ & POPULAR MUSIC

THE AMADIEAN CREED - A unique method
for creating chord voicings and
harmonizing a melody.

By Jimmy Amadie

Text and Workbook for Individual or Class Instruction

DEDICATION

*To my wife, Lucille Ann,
without whose skill in design and typing
and without whose constant support
this book would never have been completed.*

Library of Congress   Cataloging in Publication Data
Amadie, Jimmy------Harmonic foundation for jazz and popular music

1. Harmony, Keyboard. 2. Jazz music----Instruction and study. 3. Music,

Popular (Song, etc) ----Instruction and study   I.Title

MT 239.A55   1991   781.3----de19   81-670040
                              AACR 2   MARC
                                                        MN

Printed in the United States of America

International Copyright Secured

First Printing 1981
Second Printing 1991
Library of Congress   Catalog Card Number 81-670040

ISBN   0-9613035-0-6

ABOUT THE AUTHOR

Jimmy Amadie—Pianist, Composer, Arranger, Teacher and Author. Graduate of the
Philadelphia Musical Academy, BME Cum Laude, 1966

Amadie began building his reputation first as a pianist. He worked with the big band of Woody Herman and as accompanist to Mel Torme, Bobby Rydel and many other noted artists. His jazz trio played in concert with Charlie Ventura, Coleman Hawkins, Georgie Auld, and Red Rodney. Amadie was also leader of a house trio at the famous Red Hill Inn in New Jersey where many of the top jazz artists of the country would appear. His trio also played many engagements throughout the Philadelphia area. Amadie was also member of a house trio for a television station in Philadelphia. Later he brought his trio to New York's Copacabana. During the engagement he began having problems with his hands.

The condition, diagnosed as tendonitis, was a recurring problem that began during the days of his early development. With the hope of resting his hands in order to continue his career, Amadie returned to Philadelphia. However, the condition did not improve. Finally, after many years of extensive treatment, including surgery on both hands, tendonitis impaired the use of his hands.

As a result of having to play under these circumstances throughout his career, Amadie had to alter his harmonic approach, for he seldom could use all of his fingers. In reshaping his harmonic approach, and by placing emphasis on making everything count, Amadie discovered a method of determining the most important notes of a chord, and how those tones can be used with the embellished tones of a chord. He thus established a unique method for constructing chord voicings and harmonizing a melody in the modern vein.

Amadie, who has been utilizing this method in his teaching of students, teachers and professional players for twenty-five years, has clearly established a harmonic practice for modern harmony applicable to popular music, standards and jazz.

He is currently teaching Harmony, Theory and Improvisation to students and professional players, and conducting Clinic/Demonstrations, Summer Workshops, and In-Service courses for teachers at High Schools, Colleges and Universities. A former faculty member of the University of the Arts, he has taught in both Philadelphia Public and Parochial Schools as well as presented live Performing Lessons in Jazz for the Philadelphia Chapter of Young Audiences, composing over fifty compositions for the programs.

Amadie has composed for the Woody Herman Band, composed and conducted the score for the National Football League Films, co-authored compositions with Steve Allen and composed for television.

FOREWORD

"It is a pleasure and honor to write a brief foreword for Jimmy Amadie's new book, *Harmonic Foundation for Jazz and Popular Music.*

First, because Jimmy's very high level as a player, writer, teacher and complete musical person has made him <u>the</u> person to write his new book on theory and harmony. This book and his musical message are much needed and because forty percent of my "gigs" are seminars and concerts in high schools and colleges, I feel I have a unique understanding of young musicians and their needs.

It is true that this book is new and unique, using the "Amadiean Creed." However, the "Amadiean Creed" is not new – when he played for me (or anyone else) his creed was always excellence – and complete dedication to the music we were involved with.

Jimmy Amadie's *Harmonic Foundation for Jazz and Popular Music* fills some bars that should have been written some time ago – and in the right key!"

Woody Herman

FOREWORD

"In a world replete with aspiring young rock musicians, whose sole thirst for musical knowledge consists of learning the various inversions of, at the very most, four chords on a guitar, it is refreshing to know that a wonderfully talented musician, arranger, theorist – Jimmy Amadie – has taken the time to write a text on jazz harmony.

This book could not come at a better time. Currently, big bands are enjoying a true renaissance, and many young people interested in music as a career are seeking an alternative to the grinding, simplistic sameness of "today's" harmonies/melodies. For these young musicians, as well as for seasoned music-players, this new work on theory and harmony will prove invaluable.

I had the pleasure, on several occasions, of working with Jimmy Amadie. In addition to being a superb accompanist, I was struck by his originality as a solo pianist. A true original is a rarity, indeed. Amadie more than qualifies in that department. His "Amadiean Creed" found in these pages will more than attest to that.

So—Read, enjoy. And learn."

ACKNOWLEDGMENTS

Acknowledgments below are for permission to reprint excerpts from the following compositions:

"THE SHADOW OF YOUR SMILE" by J. Mandel and P. F. Webster. Copyright ©1965 Metro-Goldwyn-Mayer, Inc. All rights Administered and Controlled by Robbins Music Corporation. All rights reserved. Used by permission.

"I CAN'T GET STARTED" Words by Ira Gershwin. Music by Vernon Duke. Copyright ©1935 by Chappell & Co. Copyright renewed. International Copyright Secured. All Rights Reserved. Unauthorized copying, arranging, adapting, recording or public performance is an infringement of copyright. Infringers are liable under the law.

"LAURA" by J. Mercer and D. Raskin. Copyright ©1945, renewed 1973. Twentieth Century Music Corporation. All rights administered and controlled by Robbins Music Corporation. All rights reserved. Used by permission.

"DON'T BLAME ME" by D. Fields and J. McHugh. Copyright ©1932, renewed 1960 by Robbins Music Corporation. All rights reserved. Used by permission.

"ALL THE THINGS YOU ARE" (from "VERY WARM FOR MAY") Lyrics by Oscar Hammerstein II. Music by Jerome Kern. Copyright ©1939 PolyGram International Publishing, Inc. (3500 West Olive Avenue, Suite 200 Burbank, CA 91505) Copyright renewed. International Copyright Secured. All Rights Reserved.

"BUT BEAUTIFUL" Music by James VanHeusen. Lyrics by Johnny Burke. Copyright ©1947(renewed) Dorsey Bros. Music, a division of Music Sales Corporation and Bourne Company International. Copyright secured. All rights reserved. Used by permission.

A special thank you to Prestige Music for granting permission to use the complete composition "Tune Up" by Miles Davis. Note the copyright notice appears below the composition on pages 84 and 143.

IN APPRECIATION

Peter B. Bloom, M.D.

—a thorough professional who became a friend and whose theme of encouragement I heard clearly throughout the writing of this book.

Kent Christensen

—whose many suggestions and critical reading of preliminary drafts greatly improved the final results.

Francis Fanelli

—a pianist whose approach to a keyboard reading of this text revealed omissions and commissions in the most helpful way possible.

INTRODUCTION

The purpose of this text is to establish a foundation in modern harmony by introducing a method unique in concept and approach that will help develop the student, teacher and professional player who needs to know how to voice chords and harmonize a melody in the modern vein applicable to popular music, standards and jazz. That same harmonic foundation is the basis for jazz improvisation, composition and arranging.

The unique feature of this book is its approach. The material presented is clearly defined so not to take anything for granted. It is a practical and not theoretical method, having evolved over years of the author's own career in both playing and teaching.

The method used to establish a harmonic foundation in the modern vein and to aid the student in developing his own creativity I have chosen to call the "Amadiean Creed". The method, founded on five-note harmony, consists of two ideas: 1) embellished tones (notes that are added to a basic chord) and 2) "voicing" which I define as the position of the notes contained within the chord from the lowest note to the highest note.

In my teaching exercises, I have placed emphasis upon numerous possibilities to vary the sound of a chord by creating chord voicings and harmonizing a melody within the method. Throughout the book these principles are illustrated by discussion and exercises that deal with: 1) constructing, embellishing and voicing chords; 2) interpretation and procedure when reading chord notation; and 3) harmonization of a melody. Also, an appendix of chord voicings and an appendix of harmonized melodies are given so that the player, upon completion of his assignment in each chapter, may be afforded the opportunity to compare and evaluate his application of the method. The lessons are presented as a workbook, and if the player follows the procedure and exercises as instructed, creative development is inevitable.

Two final chapters take the method further by introducing such practical concepts as six and seven-note harmony and by offering theoretical considerations such as passing and substitute chords.

The book is planned to confront the player with situations similar to those under which he will be expected to perform. Within this frame of mind, I have attempted to simulate the player's creative ability. It is my intention to help the player develop his own talent to guide him toward self development - never to limit him.

In my experience, both pianists and non-pianists can benefit from the content of this book. For example, the responsibilities of the pianist are unlimited; he may be a soloist, he may be an accompanist, or he may be a member of a trio or a big band. This book offers the pianist the harmonic foundation that will enable him to meet these responsibilities. Also, as a teacher, I have worked with non-pianists who have found this material vital in their development of a harmonic foundation in the modern vein. For example, the composer can write in a harmonic framework and melodic framework. The arranger may orchestrate the voicings learned. The vocalist may accompany himself within the modern vein. The horn player may utilize the harmonic foundation as a background for improvisation; he may tape his own accompaniment.

The rules established in the "Amadiean Creed" are tools for creativity. This text will not limit the player's judgment and personal taste, but rather enhance them as he develops his creative ability.

The player who finishes this book will not be the same player who began it, for the world of harmony will no longer be a mystery to him. It will be a friendly world welcoming him to explore its limitless possibilities.

Jimmy Amadie

CONTENTS

APPENDIX I

APPENDIX II

CHAPTER I - MAJOR CHORDS

PART I: PREPARATION FOR VOICING MAJOR CHORDS

A. Construction of Major Chords

A major chord may be constructed by superimposing two intervals, a major 3rd and a perfect 5th, above any note. The particular note chosen is termed the "root" of the chord.

Figure 1

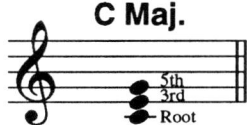

Also, in combination, the first, third, and fifth scale steps of a major scale produce a Major chord. The first scale step is termed the "root" of the Major chord.

Figure 2

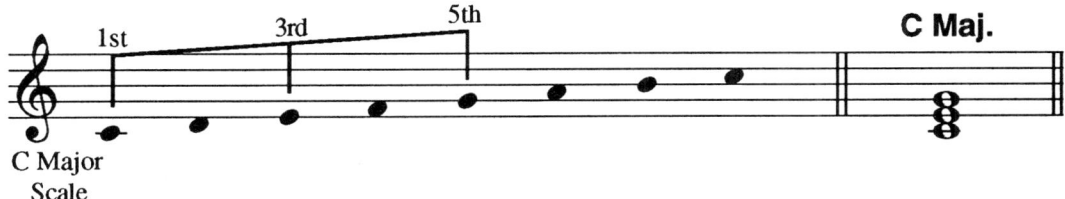

B. Embellishing a Major Chord

Added notes embellish the sound of a Major chord. In popular music, standards, and jazz, when a Major chord is indicated, it may be embellished by adding the following notes to the chord: the major 6th, major 7th and the major 9th. These notes can be used individually or in combination with the Major chord. The relationship of these added notes corresponds to the specific scale steps of that major scale as follows: Major 6th - sixth scale step above the root; major 7th - seventh scale step above the root; major 9th - ninth scale step above the root.

Figure 3

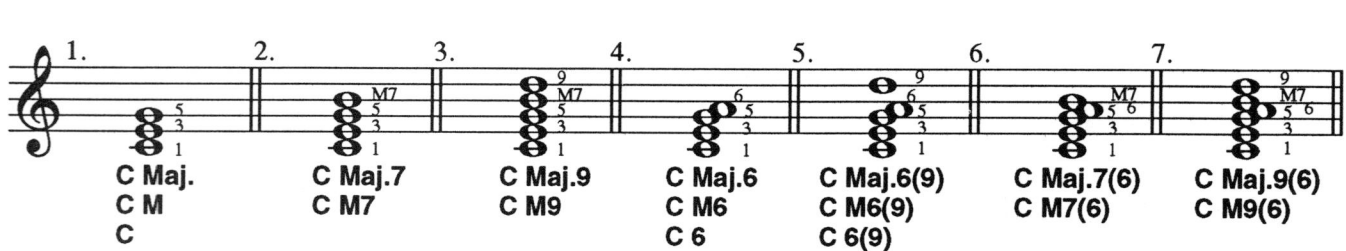

C. Notation of Major Chords

Major chords are notated as follows. Also, notice the various notations used for the same chord. (In this text the **Major 7th** is specifically indicated **M7** when the content of each chord is numerically indicated. For an example, see #2 in Figure 4 below.)

Figure 4

| 1. | 2. | 3. | 4. | 5. | 6. | 7. |

C Maj.	C Maj.7	C Maj.9	C Maj.6	C Maj.6(9)	C Maj.7(6)	C Maj.9(6)
C M	C M7	C M9	C M6	C M6(9)	C M7(6)	C M9(6)
C			C 6	C 6(9)		

Content of the above Major chords is as follows:

1. C Maj. contains the root, major 3rd above the root, and perfect 5th above the root.

2. C Maj.7 contains the root, major 3rd, perfect 5th, and major 7th.

3. C Maj.9 contains the root, major 3rd, perfect 5th, major 7th and major 9th.

4. C Maj.6 contains the root, major 3rd, perfect 5th, and major 6th.

5. C Maj.6(9) contains the root, major 3rd, perfect 5th, major 6th, and major 9th.

6. C Maj.7(6) contains the root, major 3rd, perfect 5th, major 6th and major 7th.

7. C Maj.9(6) contains the root, major 3rd, perfect 5th, major 6th, major 7th, and major 9th.

Note: Hereafter, the major 3rd, the perfect 5th, the major 6th and the major 9th will be referred to respectively as the 3rd, the 5th, the 6th and the 9th when numerically indicating the content of a major chord.

D. Bass Voicings

A "voicing" is the positioning of the notes contained within the chord from the lowest note to the highest note. At this time, we will concern ourselves with the bass voicings. A bass voicing consists of *two notes*. The bass voicings used when constructing a Major chord are as follows. **Note:** For those players not familiar with the bass clef, see Figure 5B.

Figure 5A

a. Root and 5th

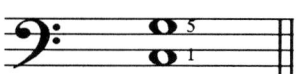

b. Root and 6th

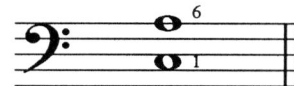

c. Root and M7th

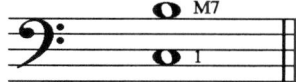

d. Root and 10th

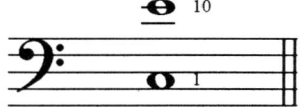

e. Optional- Root and 3rd

Note: When referring to the 10th in the bass voicing, for example, the root and 10th, we are indicating that the 3rd is being used 10 steps above the root of the chord. This applies throughout the text. Also, when the root and the 10th is beyond the player's span, use the optional root and 3rd. However, the player should strive to develop the use of both these bass voicings, especially the root and 10th.

Figure 5B

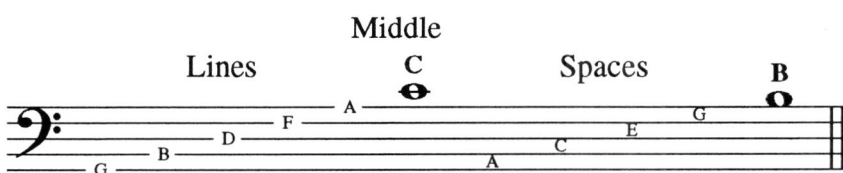

E. Rules for Voicing Major Chords

1. Use five (5) different notes when voicing a Major chord; no doubling of any note is permitted.

2. The root and 3rd must be present in the Major chord; however, the 5th can be omitted if elected to do so.

3. Embellish the chord by using the added notes indicated on page 2.

4. Omit the 5th when the maj.6th, maj.7th and maj.9th are contained in the same chord voicing so as not to exceed a total of five (5) notes in the chord voiced.

5. To begin voicing Major chords, follow the method illustrated in the "Amadiean Creed."

F. "Amadiean Creed": Method Used When Voicing Major Chords

The "Amadiean Creed" is a specific procedure--a 4 step method that enables the player to combine each phase of the material presented in letters "A" through "E" for the purpose of constructing five (5) note chord voicings. For example, Figure 6 and Figure 7 illustrate the construction of C Major chord voicings by using the step-by-step application of the method. Realize that each note is numerically indicated throughout each of the four steps so as to point out the exact relationship of each note contained in the chord.

Voicing a Major chord using the Method (for example, C Major).

Figure 6

"AMADIEAN CREED"

Step 1 (2 notes)

Select a bass voicing as illustrated in letter D. For example, the root and maj. 7th.

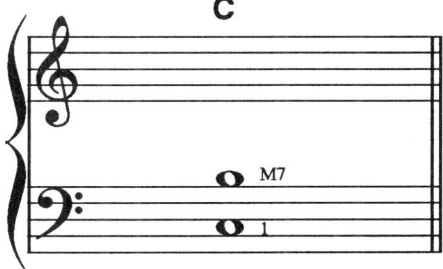

Step 2 (add 1 note)

Put the 3rd in the chord if not present in the bass voicing.

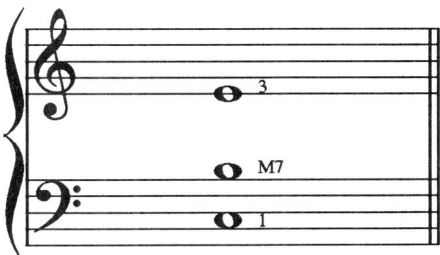

Step 3 (add 2 notes)

Complete the chord voicing by choosing two notes from those available according to the rules in letter E; here they are the 5th, maj. 6th, or the maj. 9th. The notes chosen in Figure 6 are the 5th and the maj. 9th.

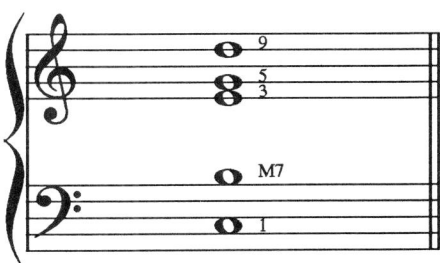

Step 4 (Notation)

Notate the chord above the staff. Realize the content of a chord determines the notation as illustrated in letter C. Realize the chord results from applying the "Amadiean Creed," which is a system for voicing chords based on a 5-note model chord containing embellished tones with no doubling.

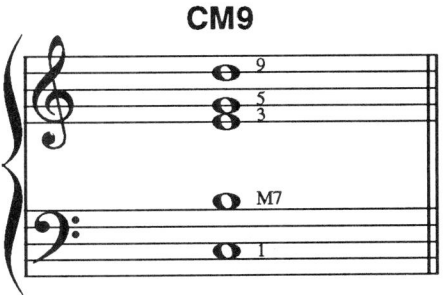

Figure 7, examples 1 and 2, illustrates the voicing of a C Maj. chord using the "Amadiean Creed." However, note **Step 1**, when the 3rd has been selected in the bass voicing, or *indicated as the 10th*. For example, root and 3rd, as in example 1, or root and 10th, as in example 2, the player needs to "adjust" **Step 2**. Furthermore, the adjustment of **Step 2**, as illustrated below, only occurs when the 3rd is selected in **Step 1**. Otherwise, **Step 2** of the "Amadiean Creed," as outlines in Figure 6, is *never* adjusted.

Figure 7

"AMADIEAN CREED"

Step 1 (2 notes)

Select a bass voicing as illustrated in letter D. For example, the root and 3rd or the root and 10th.

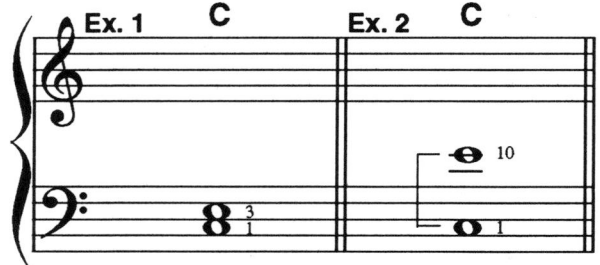

Step 2 (add 1 note)

Put the 3rd in the chord. However when the 3rd is present in the bass voicing, "adjust" **Step 2** as follows: choose one note from the available notes which are derived from the rules in letter E; here they are the 5th, maj. 6th, maj. 7th or the maj. 9th. Put the note chosen in one of the upper voices. For example, the note chosen in Figure 7 is the maj. 6th.

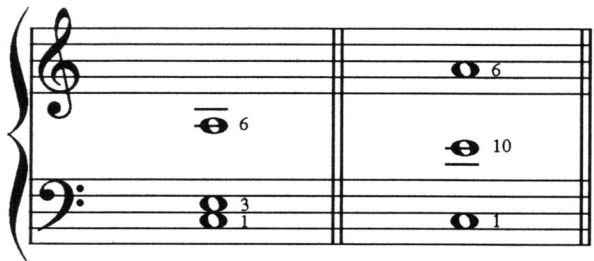

Step 3 (add 2 notes)

Complete the chord voicing by choosing two notes from the remaining notes available. For example, the notes chosen in Figure 7 are the maj. 9th, and the 5th.

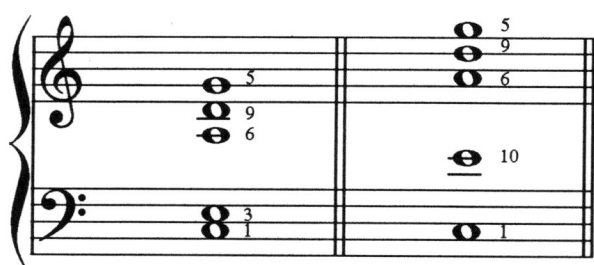

Step 4 (Notation)

Notate the chord above the staff. Realize the chord results from applying the "Amadiean Creed," which is a system for voicing chords based on a 5-note model chord with embellished tones and without doubling.

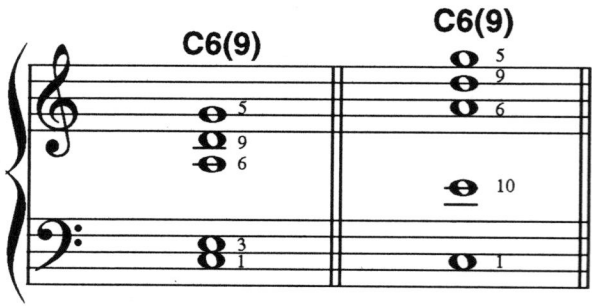

G. Examples of Major Chord Voicings

Figure 8

(musical notation: 1. GM9 2. FM9(6) 3. B♭M9 4. A♭M9(6) 5. D6(9))

H. Rules Derived From Analysis: Spacing

"Spacing" is the result of having too much distance between one voice and another within the chord thus causing the overall sound to be thin or hollow. To avoid spacing do not exceed an interval of a 7th between the 2nd and 3rd voice in the chord, also between the 3rd and 5th voice in the chord. For example, Figure 9A illustrates spacing between the 2nd voice "D" and the 3rd voice "B." The overall distance between these two notes is a 13th, the result of which produces a hollow sounding chord. However, in Figure 9B spacing is avoided as a result of not exceeding an interval of a 7th between the 2nd and 3rd voice. Realize that by moving the top three voices down an octave the content of the chord remains the same but the sound of the chord is improved.

Figure 10A illustrates "spacing" between the 3rd voice "D" and the 5th voice "E." The overall distance between these two notes is a 9th, the result of which produces a hollow sounding chord. However, in Figure 10B spacing is avoided by not exceeding an interval of a 7th between the 3rd and 5th voices. Realize that by changing the position of the 3rd voice and 5th voice in the chord, spacing is avoided and the sound of the chord is improved.

Figure 9

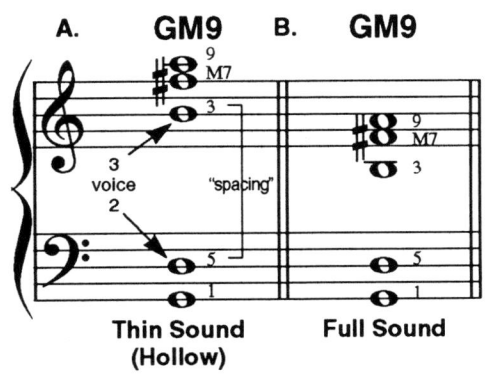

Figure 10

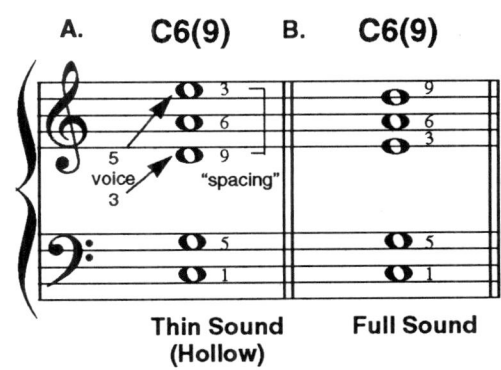

- 7 -

Now that the player has been given the background needed to construct Major chord voicings, the player is ready to apply the method. To clearly emphasize the method, the following EXERCISE I is limited to the C Major chords. However, the exercises that follow will cover all 12 Major chords.

I. ASSIGNMENT: CONSTRUCTING VOICINGS ON THE C MAJOR CHORD

Using Measure 1 as a guide, construct Major chord voicings by applying the "Amadiean Creed". Each chord must contain the exact content as indicated in the notation, also indicate the content numerically. Upon completion of the exercise, refer to *Appendix I Chord Voicings, Chapter I, Exercise I*, beginning p. 126.

"AMADIEAN CREED"   <u>EXERCISE I</u>

Step 1 (2 notes)
Select a bass voicing as indicated in letter D.

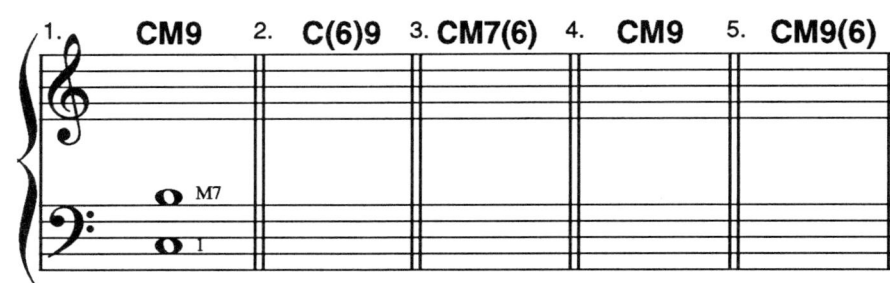

Step 2 (add 1 note)
Put the 3rd in the chord if not present in the bass voicing. However, if the 3rd is chosen in the bass voicing, see **Figure 7** (Step 2).

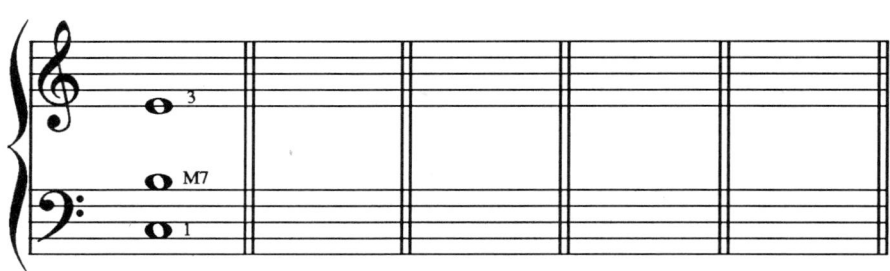

Step 3 (add 2 notes)
Complete the chord voicing as indicated in notation. Realize the two notes needed are derived from letter E, p. 4. When completed, check for "spacing."

Step 4 (Notation)
Notate the chord above the staff. Realize the chord results from applying the "Amadiean Creed": a 5-note chord voicing with no doubling. Play the chord.

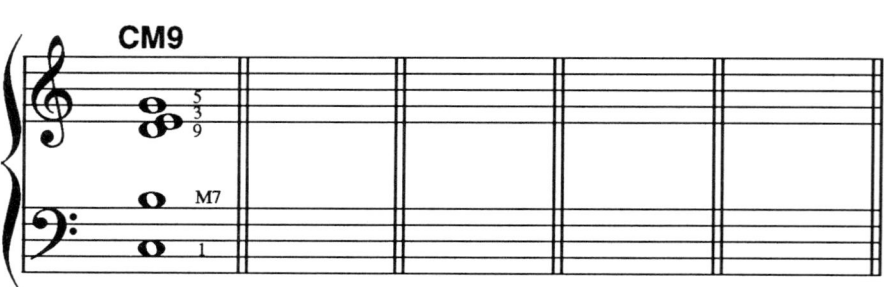

ASSIGNMENT: CONSTRUCTING VOICINGS ON THE MAJOR CHORDS

Using the voicings of your choice, construct the following Major chords as indicated in the notation. Also indicate the content of each chord as illustrated in **measure 1**. See interpretation when reading "specific chord notation" Page 10, Letter A. Upon completion of the exercise, refer to *Appendix I Chord Voicings, Chapter I, Exercise II.*

EXERCISE II

Refer to *Appendix I* as stated above before beginning the additional writing exercises.

For additional writing exercises: Construct 6 to 10 voicings of your choice using the embellished tones, according to the rules, on each of the following Major chords:

C, G, F, D, Bb, A, Eb, E, Ab, B, Db, F#, Gb, C#, Cb.

It is suggested that each assignment should consist of approximately four Major chords.

PART II: INTERPRETATION AND PROCEDURE WHEN READING MAJOR CHORD NOTATION

A. Specific Chord Notation

When reading specific chord notation of a Major chord, for example, as in EXERCISE II, Page 9, the player should use only the content of the specific chord as indicated.

B. Basic Chord Notation

When reading basic chord notation of a Major chord, for example, as in EXERCISE III, Page 11, the player is to embellish the basic chord by using the added notes as indicated on *Page 2, Letter B*.

C. Procedure for Sightreading Chord Notation in Tempo - Applying the "Amadiean Creed"

1. When sightreading chord notation, for example, as in EXERCISE III, Page 11, establish a slow tempo by counting a one measure rest.

2. As you count the measure rest in tempo, think of Steps 1, 2 and 3 of the "Amadiean Creed." Continuing in tempo, play the voicings of your choice holding each chord for 4 beats throughout the exercise.

3. When a mistake is made, Stop! Setting the tempo a little slower, count a one measure rest, allotting time to think of a voicing. Then voice the chord correctly in tempo.

The player must remember that everyone has a tempo in which he can think. Even though the tempo may be rather slow at first, the student will develop accuracy and speed as he progresses. It is unavoidable.

The purpose of this "procedure in tempo" is to help prepare the player for situations similar to those under which he will be expected to perform.

D. Assignment: Sightreading Chord Notation

In EXERCISE III, sightread the following Major chords using the added notes to embellish the basic notated chords. Follow the procedure for sightreading as indicated on *Page 10, Letter C*.

EXERCISE III

Play slowly

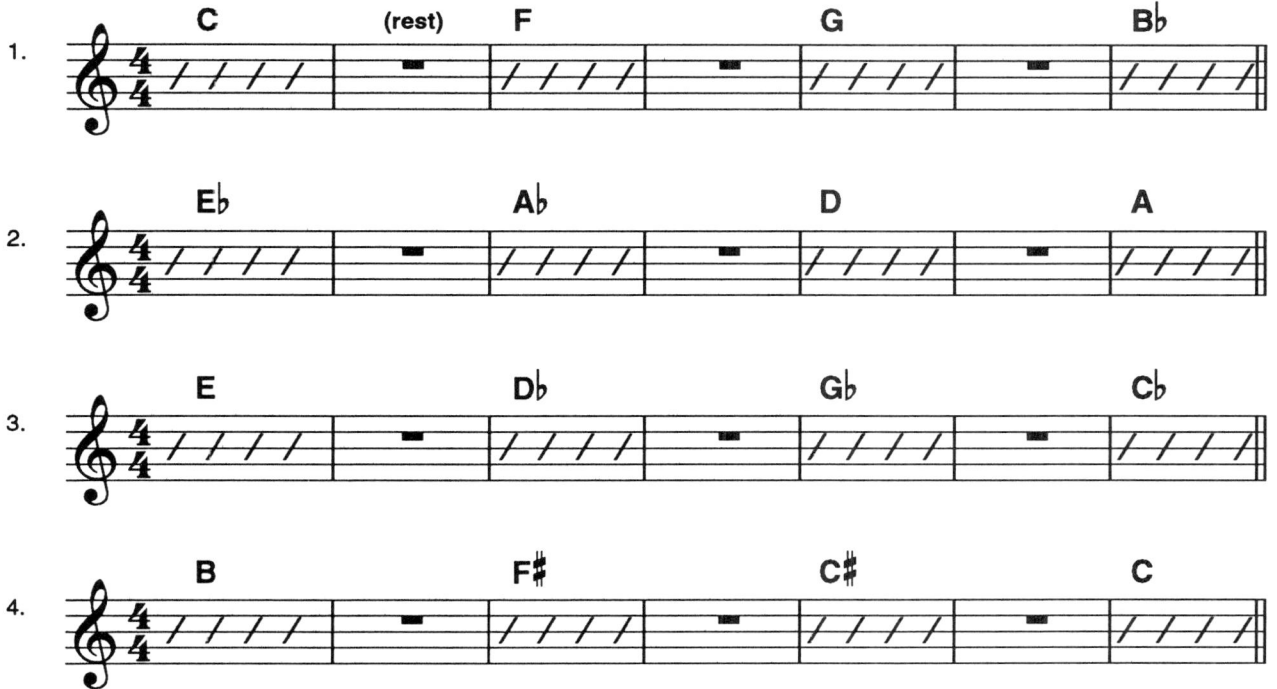

For additional sightreading exercises, read EXERCISE III in the following manner:

  1. RIGHT to LEFT (◄——) each line;
  2. From TOP to BOTTOM (↓) each column; and
  3. From BOTTOM to TOP (↑) each column.

If a player feels insecure about any particular Major chords, he may, of course, formulate different series of Major chords to overcome his weakness by stressing the more difficult ones.

PART III: INTRODUCTION TO HARMONIZATION OF A MELODY USING MAJOR CHORDS

As stated in the preface, the method used to construct a 5-note chord voicing is known as the "Amadiean Creed". This method serves as the foundation when harmonizing a melody in the modern vein. Our approach in this text is to 1) apply the method to each type of chord individually (namely: the Major, Minor, Minor 7th, Dominant 7th and the Diminished 7th chords), then, after applying the method to each type of chord, 2) harmonize a melody using each type of chord.

In addition, as we continue to apply the method to each type of chord individually, we will begin in CHAPTER 2, *PART III* to harmonize a melody by combining the various types of chords learned. As we apply the method to all chords, the player will begin to realize the full potential of the method.

Now that we have applied the method to the Major chord, we are ready to harmonize a melody using the Major chord.

A. Background for Harmonization of a Melody: The "Harmonic Change"

When harmonizing a melody, the player must understand that the "notated chord" is also known as the "harmonic change." The notated chord may appear on the beat, or on any part of the beat. In the text, the melody will be harmonized on the exact beat where the chords are notated within the composition. For example, Figure 11A indicates by the use of the bracket *left side* (⌐) the exact beat on which the melody is harmonized. Also note that the bracket encloses all the notes contained within those beats that pertain to the same harmony. For example, in Figure 11A, measure 1: the CM9 occurs on the first beat above the note "G": also realize that the following note "A" (enclosed in bracket) pertains to the CM9 harmony. Also in measure 1, the Ab6(9) occurs on the 3rd beat above the note Bb, and the following note Ab (enclosed in bracket) pertains to the Ab6(9) harmony. In measure 2, the C6(9) occurs on the first beat above the note "G", and the bracket encloses all the beats that pertain to the C6(9) harmony. (See Figures 11B and 11C for illustrations harmonizing the melody given in Figure 11A. Also, note the analysis precedes the figure.)

Figure 11A

B. Analysis of the Procedure Used to Harmonize a Melody

Analysis of Figures 11B and 11C:

1. Each chord voicing occurs on the exact beat on which the chord is notated - (harmonic change) - indicated by (↓▭) left side of bracket.

2. The melody note appears in the top voice of the chord; also, the melody note that follows remains within the framework of that same harmony (enclosed in bracket) until the new harmonic change occurs.

3. Under the given melody note, at the point where the chord is notated, a bass voicing consisting of 2 notes is inserted in the bass, indicated by (⌋).

4. Two more tones indicated by (◀▬) are added to complete the 5-note chord voicing.

5. Realize that each chord voicing contains five (5) different notes and is a reflection of the material utilized in the "Amadiean Creed."

6. Realize that the notated chords in Figure 11B and Figure 11C contain exactly the same notes; however, by changing the *voicing* of the same notated chord, realize the varied sounds which are produced.

Figure 11B

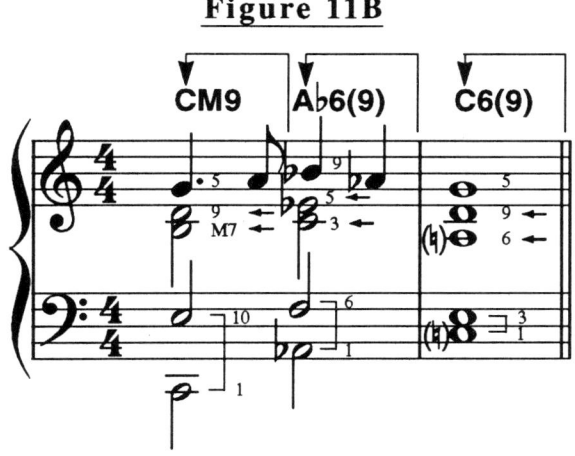

Figure 11C

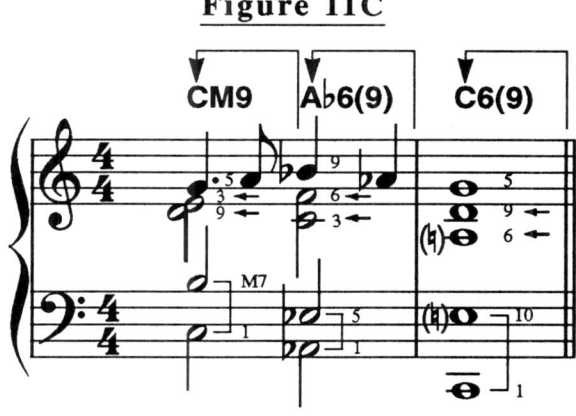

C. Special Rules for Doubling Achieved through Specific Chord Voicings

When the root or the 3rd of a major chord is the melody note, that melody note can be doubled within the 5-note chord voicing. However, the doubling of tones is limited by rules for the purpose of avoiding the sound of the basic triad and the doubling of those tones freely. This type of harmony is most often used by the inexperienced player; therefore, in utilizing the rules for doubling, "specific chord" voicings are introduced that best avoid the sound of the basic triad which results in traditional harmony and not modern harmony.

Specific Chord Voicings

For example, when the root of a Major chord is the melody note, the root can be doubled. In the examples that follow, the player should know each note contained in the specific chord voicings and then play those voicings in all the keys. Although other voicings are possible when the root is being harmonized as the melody note, in the opinion of the author, the examples given below best avoid the sound of the triad. However, after learning the specific chord voicings as suggested, the player is free to experiment on his own and adjust his voicings according to his own personal taste.

The following is an analysis of examples 1, 2, and 3 in Figure 12 when the root of a Major chord is harmonized as the melody note (top voice in the chord):

1. The root is doubled.

2. The root is doubled but also realize that the 3rd is omitted in the chord.

3. The root is omitted in the bass voicing, but the 3rd is inserted as the lowest note in the chord.

SUMMARY: It should be pointed out that in the opinion of the author, the overall quality of the chord is not disturbed by omitting the 3rd as in example 2 nor by omitting the root in the bass voicing as in example 3.

Figure 12

Root as the melody note

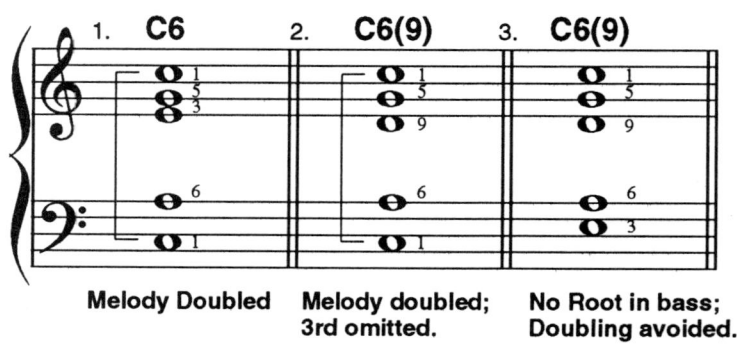

Melody Doubled   Melody doubled; 3rd omitted.   No Root in bass; Doubling avoided.

Specific Chord Voicings

When the 3rd of a major chord is the melody note, that melody note can be doubled. In the following Figure 13, specific chord voicings are illustrated. The player should know each note contained in the specific chord voicings and then play those voicings in all keys. Although other voicings are possible when the third is being harmonized as the melody note, the examples given below best avoid the sound of the basic triad. However, after learning the specific chord voicings as suggested, the player is free to experiment on his own and adjust his voicings according to his own personal taste. When the melody is doubled in the 3rd and 5th voice, as in Figure 13, "spacing" occurs, but because it is the melody note in this case, "spacing" is permitted.

Figure 13

3rd as the melody note:
melody note doubled

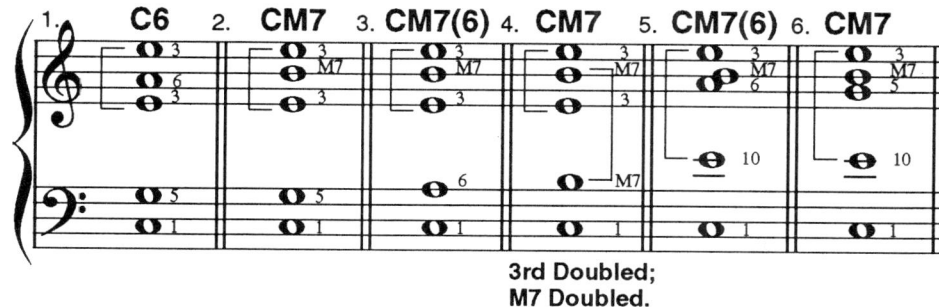

3rd Doubled;
M7 Doubled.

D. **Utilizing Specific Chord Voicings When Both the Root and the Third are the Melody Notes**

The following Figure 14 illustrates basic chords notated above the melody notes to be harmonized. However, as mentioned on page 10 letter "B", the player is to embellish the basic notated chords. See Figure 14B, examples 1 and 2 for an illustration of harmonizing a melody embellishing the basic notated chords as given in Figure 14A. Also, note the analysis precedes the Figure.

Figure 14A

Analysis of a Harmonized Melody

Analysis of Figure 14B, examples 1 and 2:

1. Realize that when harmonizing a melody, the melody is harmonized on the exact beat on which the notated chord occurs by applying Steps 1 and 3 of the method in conjunction with #2 in letter E, Rules for Voicing Major Chords (p.4).

2. Realize that the basic notated chords, as given in Figure 14A, have been embellished throughout each example in Figure 14B.

3. Notice the variety of chord voicings used throughout the examples, for instance, measures 1, 2, 3 and 4 of example 1 have different voicings when compared to the same measures in example 2.

4. Realize the use of "specific voicings" when the root is the melody note in the chord. See measure 1 in examples 1 and 2.

5. Realize the use of "specific voicings" when the 3rd is the melody note in the chord. See measure 2 and 3 in examples 1 and 2.

6. Realize that each chord voicing is a reflection of the material utilized in the "Amadiean Creed."

Figure 14B

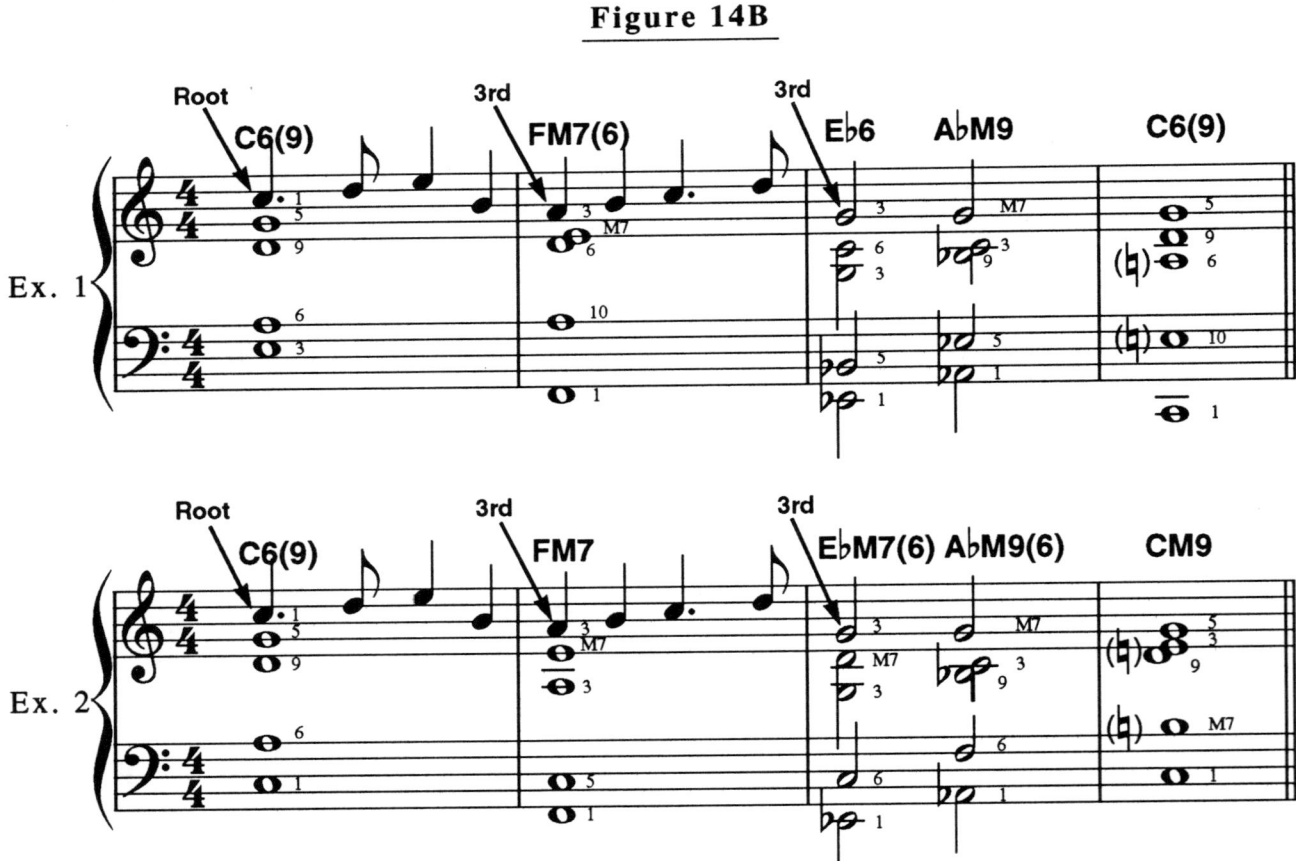

E. Melody Notes "Non-Related" to the Chord

A non-related melody note (as defined in this text) is a melody note that is not part of the basic chord nor found to be an embellished note of that chord. When a non-related note is a melody note, and that melody note appears on the beat where the notated chord occurs, harmonize that non-related note as the top voice of the chord. In addition, the non-related notes can be found as melody notes, to be harmonized, in all types of chords; namely, major, minor, minor 7th, dominant 7th and diminished 7th chords.

The following Figure 15A illustrates a melody line that contains non-related notes that are to be harmonized indicated as (indicated as N.R. in measures 2, 3 and 4 below). See Figure 15B for an illustration harmonizing non-related notes. Also, note the analysis precedes the figure.

Figure 15A

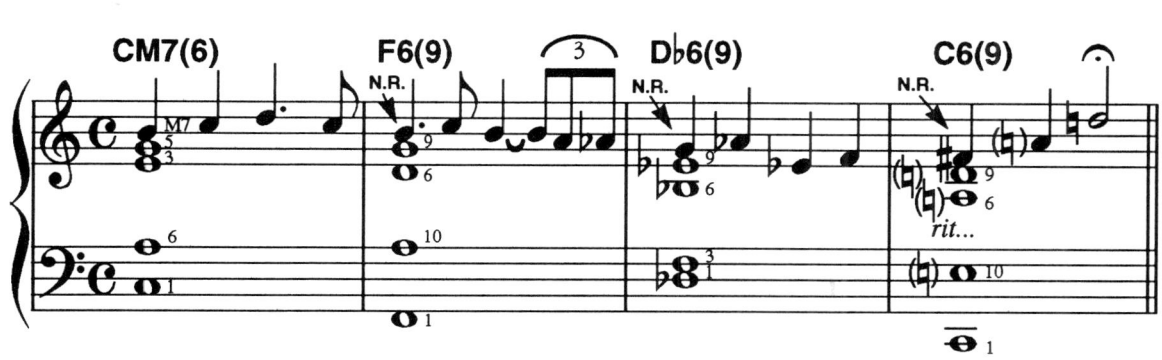

Analysis of a Harmonized Melody

1. Realize that Figure 15B is an illustration of harmonizing the melody given in Figure 15A.

2. Realize that the basic notated chords, as given in Figure 15A, have been embellished in Figure 15B.

3. Realize that non-related melody notes are harmonized in measures 2, 3 and 4.

4. Realize that each chord voicing is a reflection of the material utilized in the "Amadiean Creed."

Figure 15B

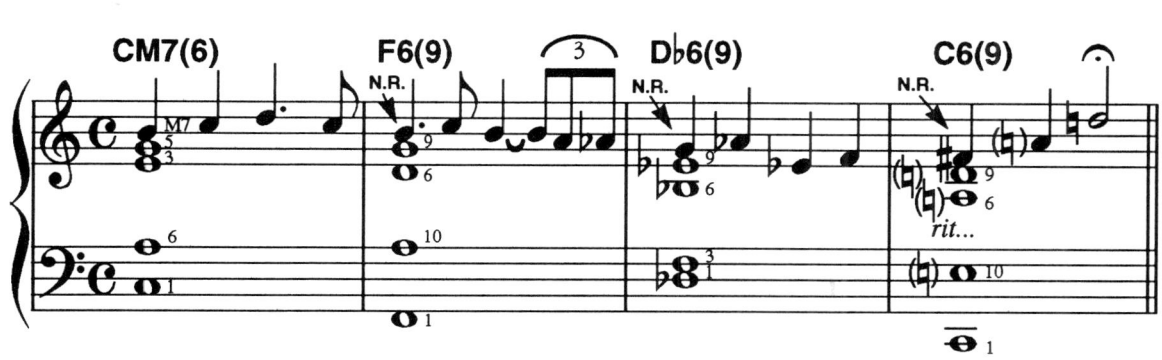

F.   Assignment: *Harmonizing Melodies Using Major Chords*

Exercises 1 through 5

In the following Exercises 1 through 5, the melody lines are specifically designed for the purpose of applying the "method" when harmonizing a melody using the Major chords. Upon completion of the exercise, refer to *Appendix II Harmonized Melodies, Chapter I, Exercises 1 through 5*, beginning p. 136.

Harmonize the melodies in the following exercises embellishing the basic notated chords. The embellished chords must be notated above the basic chord where indicated in notation. Also indicate the content of each chord numerically. N.R. designates "non-related" melody notes in the exercises; these notes should not be indicated numerically or included in the notation of the chord. For purposes of the exercises, play in a slow to moderate tempo.

SUMMARY: This uniquely organized method and approach to harmony combines rules for constructing chord voicings with rules for harmonizing a melody. As previously stated, the format of this text deals with each type of chord individually before applying the method to all types of chords. With this in mind, let us continue to progress by moving on to the next chord: the Minor Chord.

CHAPTER II - MINOR CHORDS

PART I: PREPARATION FOR VOICING MINOR CHORDS

A. Construction of Minor Chords

A Minor chord may be constructed by superimposing two intervals, a minor 3rd and a perfect 5th, above any note. The particular note chosen is termed the "root" of the chord.

Figure 16

Also, in combination, the first, third, and fifth scale steps of an **ascending** melodic minor scale produce a Minor chord. The first scale step is termed the "root" of the Minor chord.

Figure 17

B.   Embellishing a Minor Chord

Added notes embellish the sound of a Minor chord. In popular music, standards, and jazz, when a Minor chord is indicated, it may be embellished by adding the following notes to the chord: the major 6th, major 7th and the major 9th. These notes can be used individually or in combination with the Minor chord. The relationship of these added notes corresponds to the specific scale steps of that **ascending** melodic Minor scale as follows: major 6th - sixth scale step above the root; major 7th - seventh scale step above the root; major 9th - ninth scale step above the root.

Figure 18

C.   Notation of Minor Chords

Minor chords are notated as follows. Also, notice the various notations used for the same chord. In addition, the major 7th, when indicated in notation, can be indicated in various ways: for example, (M7), (+7), ($\sharp$7). For an example, see Figure 19, #2. For consistency, we have chosen to use the symbol (M7) in notation throughout the text, as in #3.

Figure 19

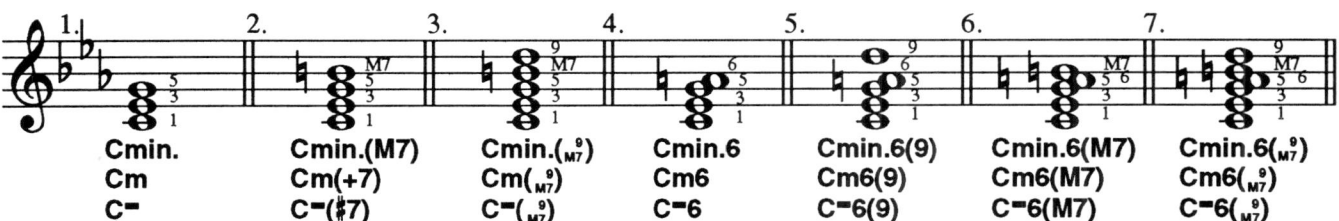

Content of the above Minor chords is as follows:

1.   C Min. contains the root, minor 3rd above the root, and perfect 5th above the root.

2.   C Min.(M7) contains the root, minor 3rd, perfect 5th, and major 7th.

3.   C Min.($_{M7}^{9}$) contains the root, minor 3rd, perfect 5th, major 7th and major 9th.

4. C min.6 contains the root, minor 3rd, perfect 5th, and major 6th.

5. C min.6(9) contains the root, minor 3rd, perfect 5th, major 6th, and major 9th.

6. C min.6(M7) contains the root, minor 3rd, perfect 5th, major 6th and major 7th.

7. C min.6($^{9}_{M7}$) contains the root, minor 3rd, perfect 5th, major 6th, major 7th, and major 9th.

Note: Hereafter, the minor 3rd, the perfect 5th, the major 6th and the major 9th will be referred to respectively as the 3rd, the 5th, the 6th and the 9th when numerically indicating the content of a minor chord.

D. Bass Voicings

A bass voicing consists of two notes. The bass voicings used when constructing a minor chord are as follows:

Figure 20

a. Root and 5th

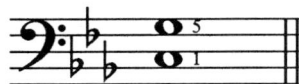

b. Root and 6th

c. Root and M7th

d. Root and 10th

e. Optional - Root and 3rd

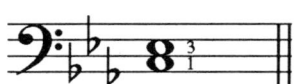

E. Rules for Voicing Minor Chords

1. Use five (5) different notes when voicing a Minor chord; no doubling of any note is permitted.
2. The root and 3rd must be present in the Minor chord; however, the 5th can be omitted if elected to do so.
3. Embellish the chord by using the added notes indicated on page 21.
4. Omit the 5th when the maj.6th, maj.7th and maj.9th are contained in the same chord voicing so as not to exceed a total of five (5) notes in the chord voiced.
5. To begin voicing Minor chords, follow the method illustrated in the "Amadiean Creed."

F. "Amadiean Creed": Method Used When Voicing Minor Chords

The method used to voice Minor Chords is the "Amadiean Creed". The following examples, Figure 21 and Figure 22, illustrate the construction of C min. chord voicings by using the step-by-step application of the method. Realize that each note is numerically indicated throughout each of the four steps so as to point out the exact relationship of each note contained in the chord.

Voicing a Minor chord using the Method (for example, C Minor).

Figure 21

"AMADIEAN CREED"

Step 1 (2 notes)

Select a bass voicing as illustrated in letter D. For example, the root and 5th.

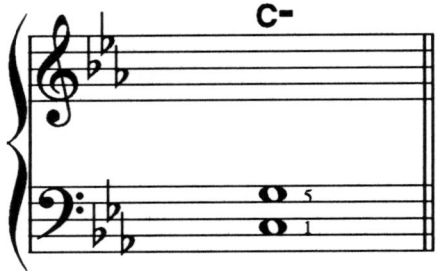

Step 2 (add 1 note)

Put the 3rd in the chord if not present in the bass voicing.

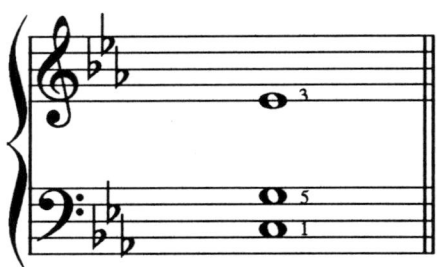

Step 3 (add 2 notes)

Complete the chord voicing by choosing two notes from those available according to the rules in letter E; here they are the maj. 6th, maj. 7th or the maj. 9th. The notes chosen in Figure 21 are the maj. 6th and the maj. 9th.

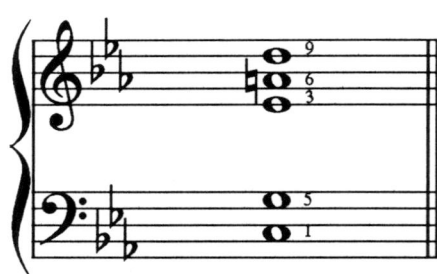

Step 4 (Notation)

Notate the chord above the staff. Realize the chord results from applying the "Amadiean Creed," which is a system for voicing chords based on a 5-note model chord containing embellished tones with no doubling.

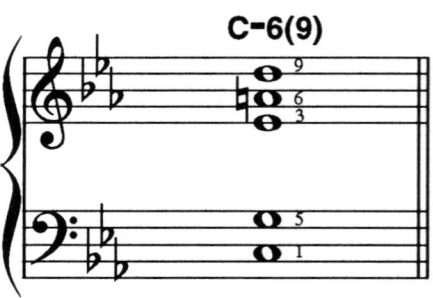

Figure 22, examples 1 and 2, illustrates the voicing of a C Minor chord using the "Amadiean Creed." However, note **Step 1**, when the 3rd has been selected in the bass voicing, or *indicated as the 10th*. For example, root and 3rd, as in example 1, or root and 10th, as in example 2, the player needs to "adjust" **Step 2**. Furthermore, the adjustment of **Step 2**, as illustrated below, only occurs when the 3rd is selected in **Step 1**. Otherwise, **Step 2** of the "Amadiean Creed," as outlined in Figure 21, is *never* adjusted.

Figure 22

"AMADIEAN CREED"

Step 1 (2 notes)

Select a bass voicing as illustrated in letter D. For example, the root and 3rd or the root and 10th.

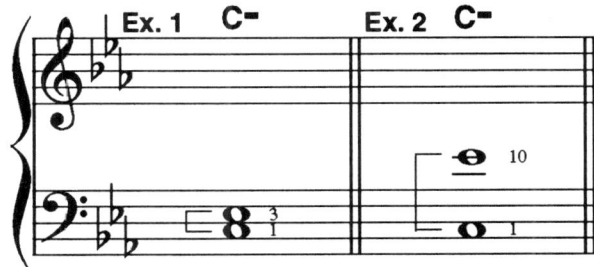

Step 2 (add 1 note)

Put the 3rd in the chord. However when the 3rd is present in the bass voicing, "adjust" **Step 2** as follows: choose one note from the available notes which are derived from the rules in letter E; here they are the 5th, maj. 6th, maj. 7th or the maj. 9th. Put the note chosen in one of the upper voices. For example, the note chosen in Figure 22 is the maj. 6th.

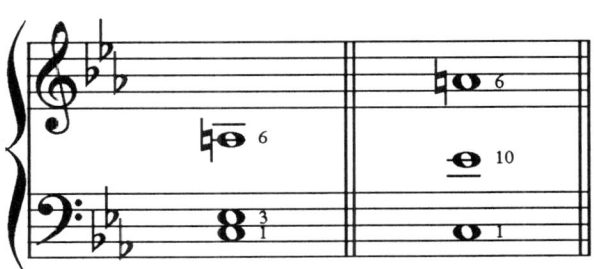

Step 3 (add 2 notes)

Complete the chord voicing by choosing two notes from the remaining notes available. For example, the notes chosen in Figure 22 are the maj. 9th and the 5th.

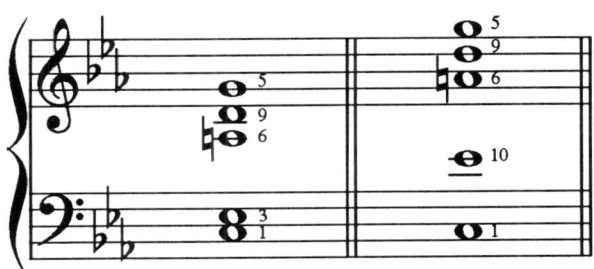

Step 4 (Notation)

Notate the chord above the staff. Realize the chord results from applying the "Amadiean Creed," which is a system for voicing chords based on a 5-note model chord with embellished tones and without doubling.

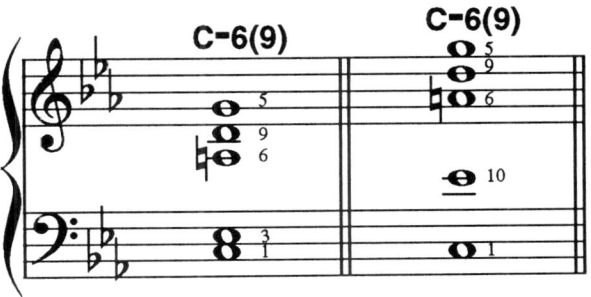

G. Examples of Minor Chord Voicings

Figure 23

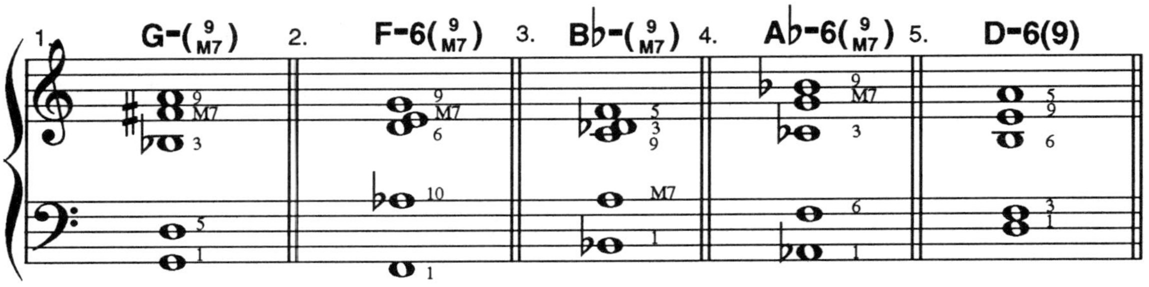

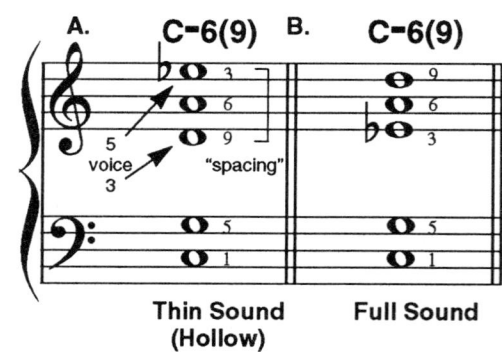

H. Rules Derived From Analysis: Spacing

"Spacing" (as mentioned on page 7) is the result of having too much distance between one voice and another within the chord, thus causing the sound to be thin or hollow. To avoid spacing do not exceed an interval of a 7th between the 2nd and 3rd voice in the chord, also between the 3rd and 5th voice of the chord. For example, Figure 24A illustrates spacing between the 2nd voice "D" and the 3rd voice "B♭." The overall distance between these two notes is a -13th, the result of which produces a hollow sounding chord; however, in Figure 24B spacing is avoided as a result of not exceeding an interval of a 7th between the 2nd and 3rd voice. Realize that by moving the top three voices down an octave, the content of the chord remains the same, but the sound of the chord is improved.

Figure 25A illustrates "spacing" between the 3rd voice "D" and the 5th voice "E♭." The overall distance between these two notes is a -9th, the result of which produces a hollow sounding chord; however, in Figure 25B spacing is avoided by not exceeding an interval of a 7th between the 3rd and 5th voice. Realize that by changing the position of the 3rd voice and the 5th voice of the chord, spacing is avoided and the sound of the chord is improved.

Figure 24   Figure 25

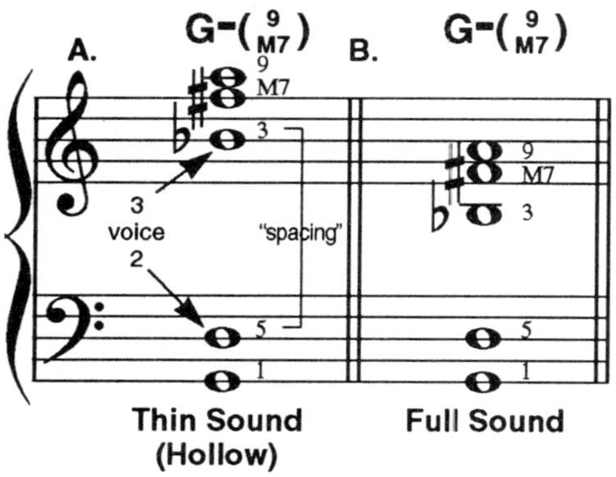

Now that the player has been given the background needed to construct Minor chord voicings, the player is ready to apply the method. To clearly emphasize the method, the following EXERCISE I is limited to the C Minor chords. However, the exercises that follow will cover all 12 Minor chords.

I.   ASSIGNMENT: CONSTRUCTING VOICINGS ON THE C MINOR CHORD

Using Measure 1 as a guide, construct Minor chord voicings by applying the "Amadiean Creed." Each chord must contain the exact content as indicated in the notation, also indicate the content numerically. You should realize that when they are isolated, as in this exercise, minor chords may sound dissonant. But, when heard in the proper context, they will become effective as you will see in the examples at the end of this chapter and elsewhere in the text. Upon completion of the exercise, refer to *Appendix I Chord Voicings, Chapter II, Exercise I*.

"AMADIEAN CREED"   **EXERCISE I**

Step 1 (2 notes)
Select a bass voicing as indicated in letter D.

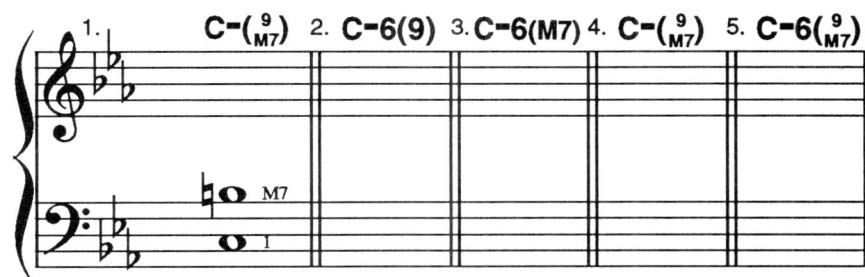

Step 2 (add 1 note)
Put the 3rd in the chord if not present in the bass voicing. However, if the 3rd is chosen in the bass voicing, see **Figure 22** (Step 2).

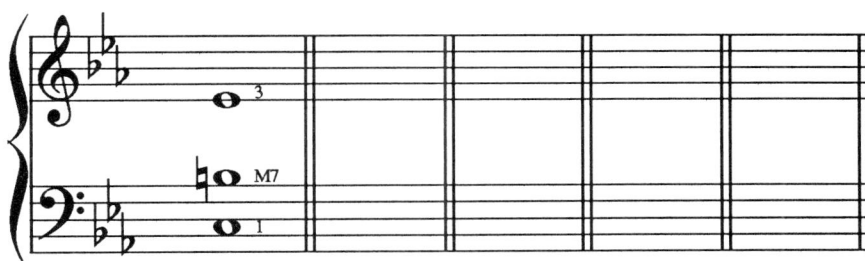

Step 3 (add 2 notes)
Complete the chord voicing as indicated in notation. Realize the two notes needed are derived from letter E, p.23. When completed, check for "spacing".

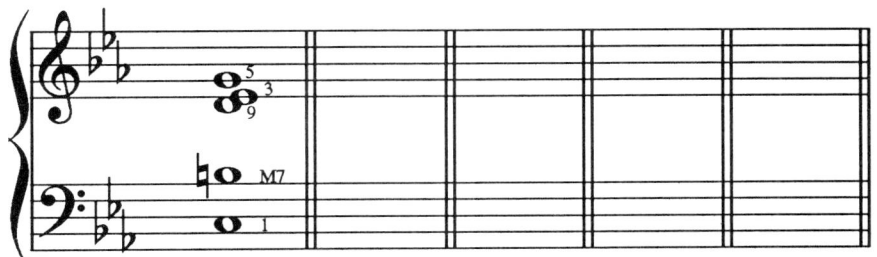

Step 4 (Notation)
Notate the chord above the staff. Realize the chord results from applying the "Amadiean Creed": a 5-note chord voicing with no doubling. Play the chord.

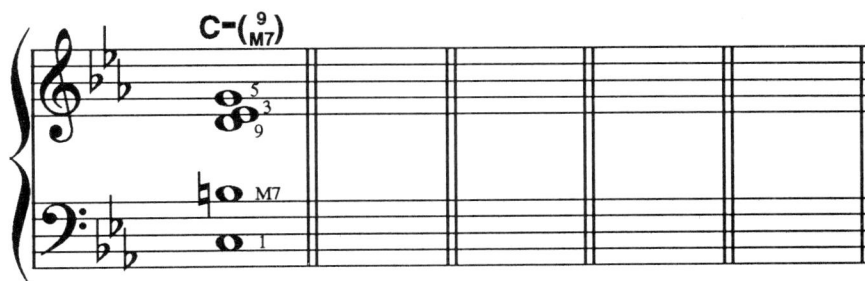

ASSIGNMENT: CONSTRUCTING VOICINGS ON THE MINOR CHORDS

Using the voicings of your choice, construct the following Minor chords as indicated in the notation. Also indicate the content of each chord as illustrated in *measure 1*. See interpretation when reading "specific chord notation" Page 29, Letter A. Upon completion of the exercise, refer to *Appendix I Chord Voicings, Chapter II, Exercise II*.

EXERCISE II

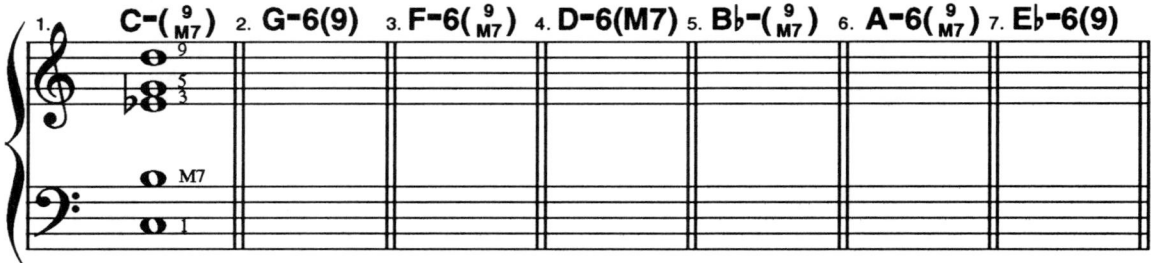

Refer to *Appendix I* as stated above before beginning the additional writing exercises.

For additional writing exercises: Construct 6 to 10 voicings of your choice using the embellished tones, according to the rules, on each of the following Minor chords:

C-, G-, F-, D-, B♭-, A-, E♭-, E-, A♭-, B-, D♭-, F♯-, G♭-, C♯-, C♭-.

It is suggested that each assignment should consist of approximately four Minor chords.

PART II: INTERPRETATION AND PROCEDURE WHEN READING MINOR CHORD NOTATION

A. Specific Chord Notation

When reading specific chord notation of a Minor chord, for example, as in EXERCISE II, Page 28, the player should use only the content of the specific chord as indicated.

B. Basic Chord Notation

When reading basic chord notation of a Minor chord, for example, as in EXERCISE III, Page 30, the player is to embellish the basic chord by using the added notes as indicated on *Page 21, Letter B*.

C. Procedure for Sightreading Chord Notation in Tempo - Applying the "Amadiean Creed"

1. When sightreading chord notation, establish a slow tempo by counting a one measure rest.

2. As you count the measure rest in tempo, think of Steps 1, 2 and 3 of the "Amadiean Creed." Continuing in tempo, play the voicings of your choice holding each chord for 4 beats throughout the exercise.

3. When a mistake is made, Stop! Setting the tempo a little slower, count a one measure rest, allotting time to think of a voicing. Then voice the chord correctly in tempo.

D. Assignment: Sightreading Chord Notation

In Exercise III, sightread the following Minor chords using the added notes to embellish the basic notated chords. Follow the procedure for sightreading as indicated on *Page 29, Letter C.*

EXERCISE III

Play slowly

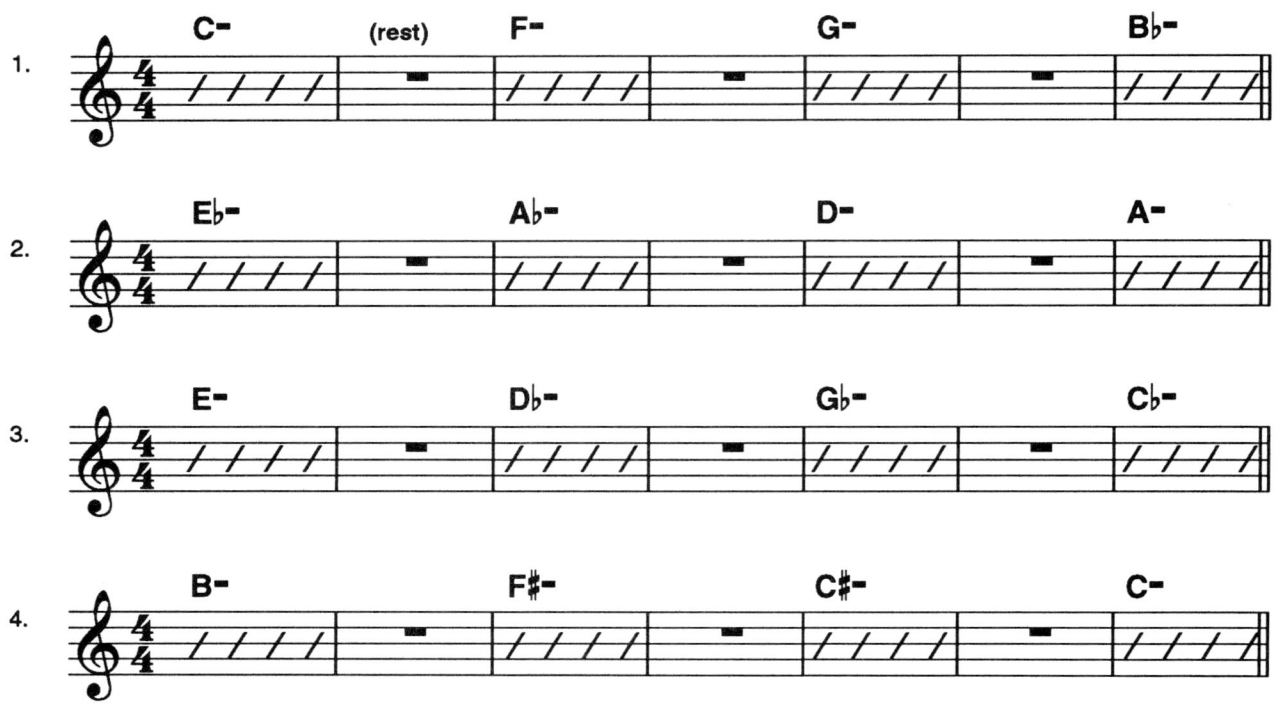

For additional sightreading exercises, read EXERCISE III in the following manner:

1. RIGHT TO LEFT (◄——) each line;
2. From TOP to BOTTOM (▼) each column; and
3. From BOTTOM to TOP (▲) each column.

If a player feels insecure about any particular Minor chords, he may, of course, formulate different series of Minor chords to overcome his weakness by stressing the more difficult ones.

PART III: INTRODUCTION TO HARMONIZATION OF A MELODY USING MAJOR AND MINOR CHORDS

Now that we have applied the method of constructing 5-note chord voicings to Minor chords, we are ready to harmonize a melody using the Minor chords. Also, in the examples that follow, melodies are harmonized utilizing the various types of chords learned thus far; namely, the Major and Minor chords.

A. Background for Harmonization of a Melody: The "Harmonic Change"

As previously stated in Chapter I, PART III, a "notated chord" is also known as the "harmonic change." Let us continue to apply the same principle. For example, when harmonizing a melody, the melody will be harmonized on the exact beat on which the "notated chords" occur indicated by the *left side* of the bracket (⌐). Also, note that the bracket encloses all the notes contained within those beats that pertain to the same harmony. For example, in Figure 26A, measure 1: the C-6(9) occurs on the first beat above the note G; also realize that the following note A (enclosed in bracket) pertains to the C-6(9)harmony. Also in measure 1, the Ab-6(9) occurs on the third beat above the note Bb, and the following note Ab (enclosed in bracket) pertains to the Ab-6(9) harmony. In measure 2, the C-6(9) occurs on the first beat above the note G, and the bracket encloses all the beats that pertain to the C-6(9) harmony. See Figures 26B and 26C for illustrations harmonizing the melody given in Figure 26A. Also note the analysis precedes the figure.

Figure 26A

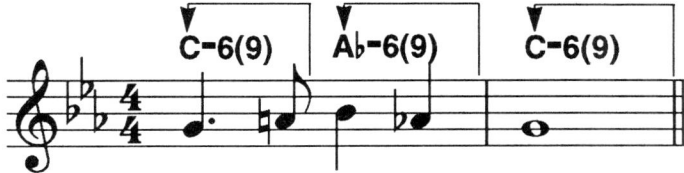

B. Analysis of the Procedure Used to Harmonize a Melody

Analysis of Figures 26B and 26C:

1. Each chord voicing occurs on the exact beat on which the chord is notated; (harmonic change) - indicated by (▼‾‾‾‾|) left side of bracket.

2. The melody note appears in the top voice of the chord; also, the melody note that follows remains within the framework of that same harmony (enclosed in bracket) until the new harmonic change occurs.

3. Under the given melody note, at the point where the chord is notated, a bass voicing consisting of two notes is inserted in the bass, indicated by ( ]).

4. Two more tones indicated by (⇐) are added to complete the 5-note chord voicing.

5. Realize that the notated chords in Figures 26B and 26C contain exactly the same notes; however, by changing the voicing of the same notated chord, realize the varied sounds which are produced.

6. Realize that each chord voicing contains five (5) different notes and is a reflection of the material utilized in the "Amadiean Creed."

Figure 26B

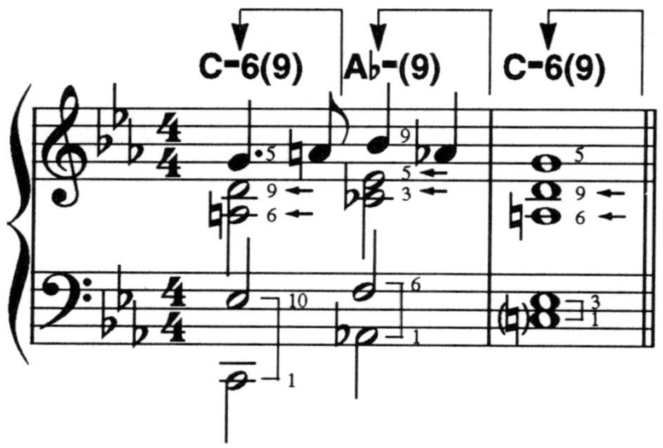

Figure 26C

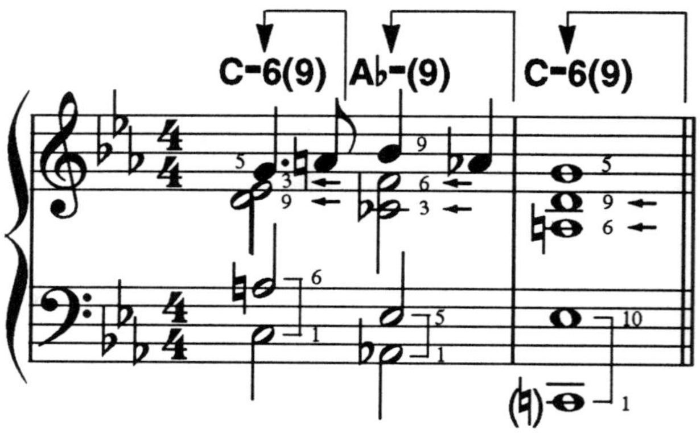

C. Special Rules for Doubling Achieved through Specific Chord Voicings

When the root or the 3rd of a minor chord is the melody note, that melody note can be doubled within the 5-note chord voicing. However, the doubling of tones, as previously explained in PART III, letter "C" of Major chords, is limited by utilizing specific chord voicings that best avoid the sound of the basic triad.

Specific Chord Voicings

For example, when the root of a Minor chord is the melody note, the root can be doubled. In the examples that follow, the player should know each note contained in the specific chord voicings and then play those voicings in all keys. Although other voicings are possible when the root is being harmonized as the melody note in a Minor chord, in the opinion of the author, the examples given below best avoid the sound of the basic triad. However, after learning the specific chord voicings as suggested, the player is free to experiment on his own and adjust his voicings according to his own personal taste.

The following is an analysis of examples 1, 2, 3 and 4 in Figure 27 when the root of a Minor chord is harmonized as the melody note:

1. The root is doubled.

2. The root is doubled.

3. The root is doubled, and the 6th is doubled.

4. The root is omitted in the bass voicing, but the 3rd is inserted as the lowest note in the chord.

SUMMARY: It should be pointed out that in the opinion of the author, the overall quality of the chord is not disturbed by omitting the root in the bass voicing, as in example 4 of Figure 27.

Figure 27

Root as the melody note

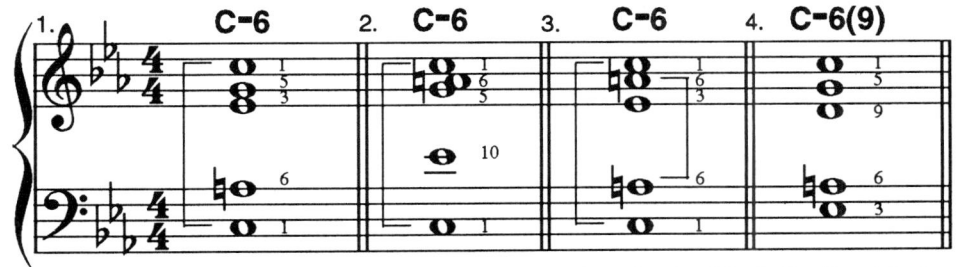

Melody doubled;   Melody doubled;   Melody doubled;   No Root in bass;
6th doubled.   doubling avoided.

Specific Chord Voicings

When the 3rd of a minor chord is the melody note, that melody note can be doubled. In the following Figure 28, specific chord voicings are illustrated. The player should know each note contained in the specific chord voicings and then play those voicings in all the keys. As previously explained, the examples given below best avoid the sound of the basic triad. However, after learning the specific chord voicings as suggested, the player is free to experiment on his own and adjust his voicings according to his own personal taste.

Note: "Spacing" is permitted only when the melody is doubled in the 3rd and 5th voice.

Figure 28

3rd as the melody note; melody note doubled.

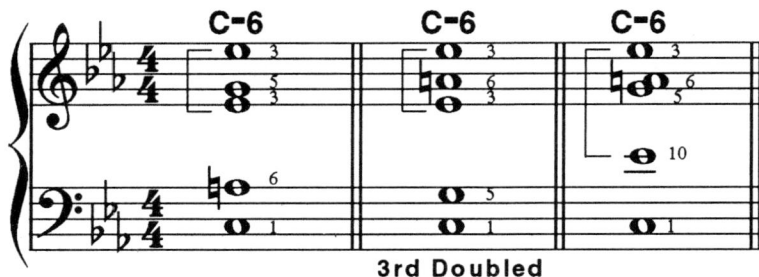

3rd Doubled

D. Utilizing Specific Chord Voicings When Both the Root and the Third are the Melody Notes

The following Figure 29A illustrates basic chords notated above melody notes to be harmonized. However, as mentioned on page 29, letter "B", the player is to embellish the basic notated chords. See Figure 29B, examples 1 and 2, for an illustration of harmonizing a melody embellishing the basic notated chords as given in Figure 29A. Also note analysis precedes the figure.

Figure 29A

Analysis of a Harmonized Melody

Analysis of Figure 29B, examples 1 and 2:

1.   Realize that when harmonizing a melody, the melody is harmonized on the exact beat on which the notated chord occurs by applying Steps 1 and 3 of the "method" in conjunction with #2 in letter E, Rules for Voicing Minor Chords (p.23).

2.   Realize that the basic notated chords, as given in Figure 29A, have been embellished throughout each example in Figure 29B.

3.   Realize the variety of chord voicings used throughout the examples; for instance, in comparing measures 1, 2, 3, 4 and 5 of examples 1 and 2, each voicing is different.

4.   Realize the use of "specific chord voicings" when the root is the melody note in the chord. See measures 1 and 2 in examples 1 and 2.

5.   Realize the use of "specific chord voicings" when the 3rd is the melody note in the chord. See measure 3 in examples 1 and 2.

6.   Realize that each chord voicing is a reflection of the material utilized in the "Amadiean Creed."

Figure 29B

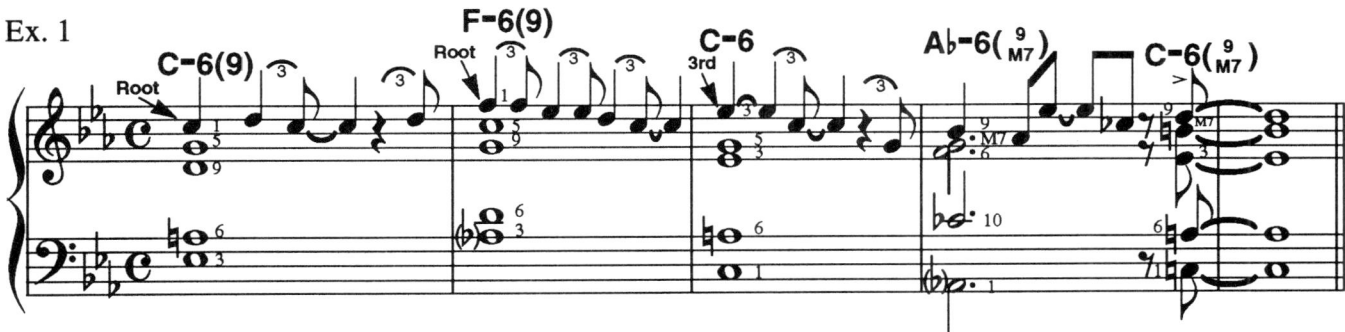

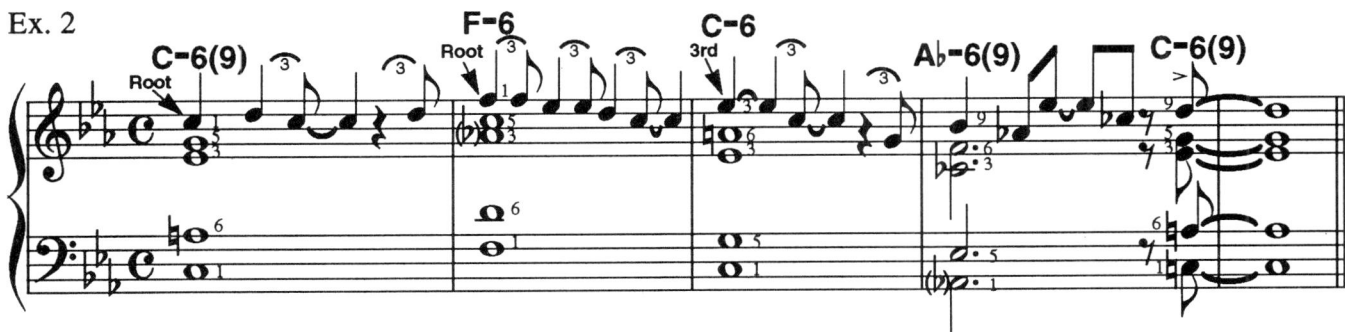

E. Melody Notes "Non-Related" to the Chord

A non-related melody note (as previously defined in CHAPTER I, PART III) is a melody note that is not part of the basic chord or found to be an embellished note of that chord.

The following Figure 30A illustrates a melody line that contains non-related notes that are to be harmonized (see measure 1 and 3). See Figure 30B for an illustration harmonizing non-related notes. Also note the analysis precedes the figure.

Figure 30A

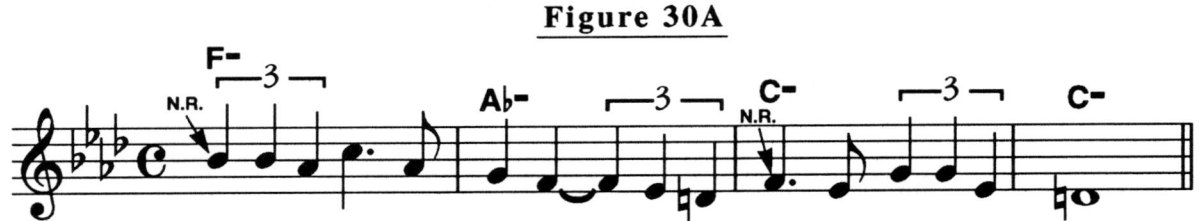

Analysis of a Harmonized Melody

1. Realize that Figure 30B is an illustration of harmonizing the melody given in Figure 30A.

2. Realize that the basic notated chords, as given in Figure 30A, have been embellished in Figure 30B.

3. Realize that non-related melody notes are harmonized in measures 1 and3.

4. Realize that each chord voicing is a reflection of the material utilized in the "Amadiean Creed."

Figure 30B

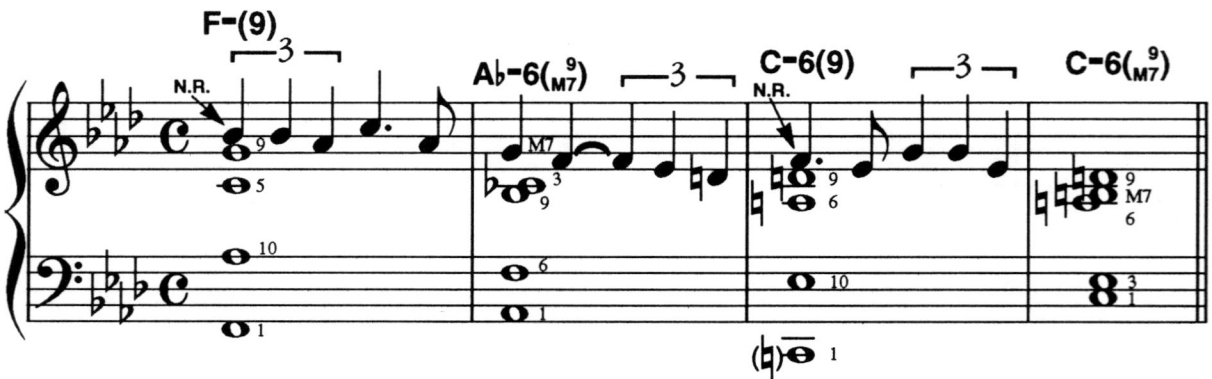

F. Assignment: Harmonizing Melodies Using Major and Minor Chords

Exercises 1 through 5

In the following Exercises 1 through 5, the melody lines are specifically designed for the purpose of applying the "method" when harmonizing a melody using Major and Minor chords. Upon completion of the exercise refer to *Appendix II Harmonized Melodies, Chapter II, Exercises 1 through 5.*

Harmonize the melodies in the following exercises embellishing the basic notated chords. The embellished chords must be notated above the basic chord where indicated in notation. Also indicate the content of each chord numerically. The Non-Related melody notes are indicated "N.R." For purposes of the exercises, play in a slow to moderate tempo.

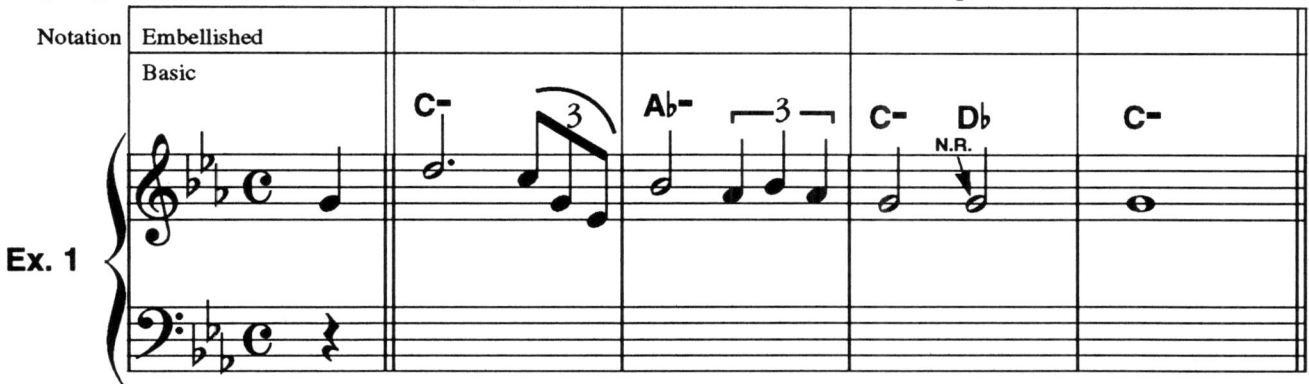

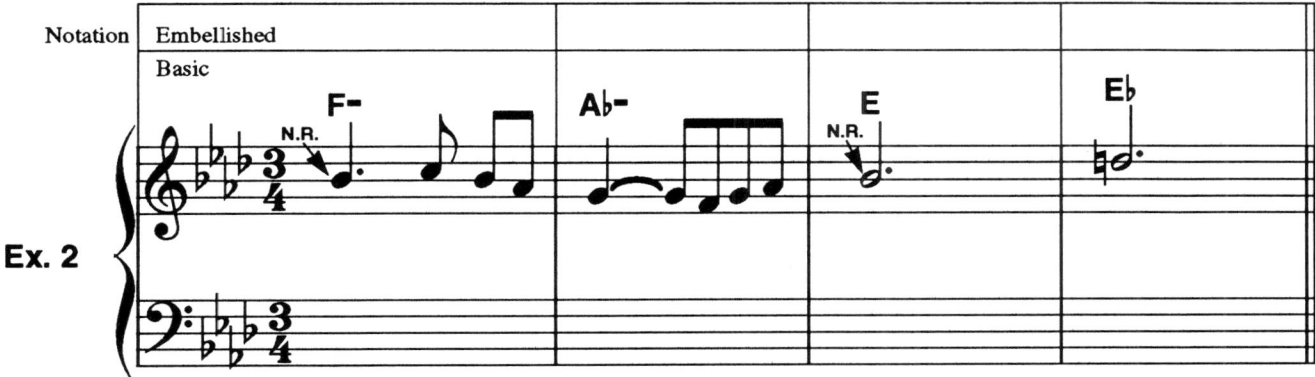

SUMMARY: It should be obvious that the method used to construct chord voicings and the utilization of that method when harmonizing a melody is exactly the same for both Major and Minor chords. Let us continue to progress by moving on to the next chord: the Minor 7th chord.

CHAPTER III - MINOR 7TH CHORDS

PART I: PREPARATION FOR VOICING MINOR 7TH CHORDS

A.   Construction of Minor 7th Chords

A Minor 7th chord may be constructed by superimposing three intervals, a minor 3rd and a perfect 5th, and a minor 7th above any note.   The particular note chosen is termed the "root" of the chord.

Figure 31

Also, a Minor 7th chord can be constructed on the 2nd degree of a major scale by combining that degree termed "root" (1) of the chord, and the following degrees located above that "root"; a 3rd, a 5th and 7th.

Figure 32

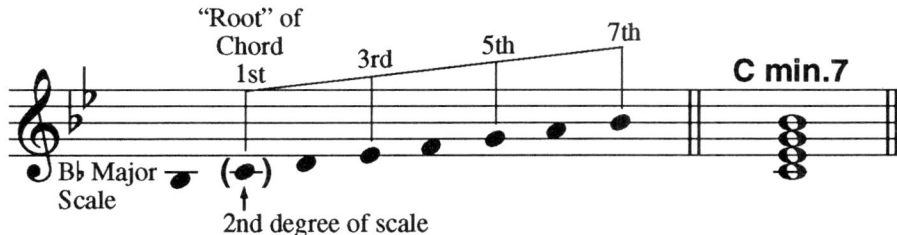

B.   Embellishing a Minor 7th Chord

Added notes embellish the sound of a Minor 7th chord. In popular music, standards, and jazz, when a Minor 7th chord is indicated, it may be embellished by adding the following notes to the chord: the major 9th and the perfect 11th. These notes can be used individually or in combination with the Minor 7th chord. Considering the root as the 1st degree of the chord, the added notes are computed above that "root." For example, the major 9th - ninth step above the root; the perfect 11th - eleventh step above the root.

Figure 33

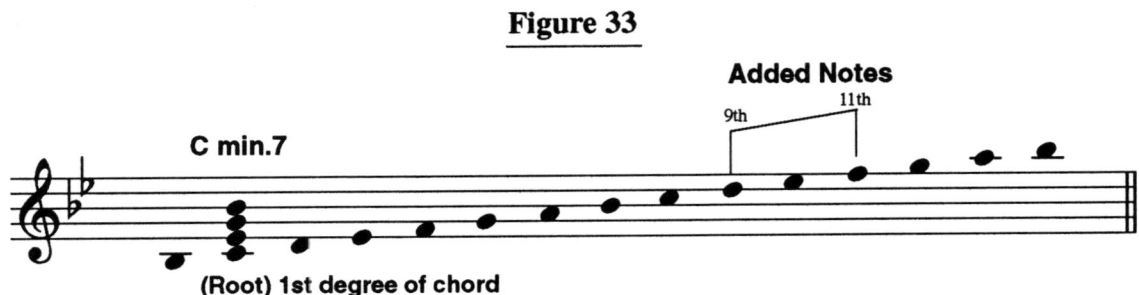

C.   Notation of Minor 7th Chords

Minor 7th chords are notated as follows. Also, notice the various notations used for the same chord.

Figure 34

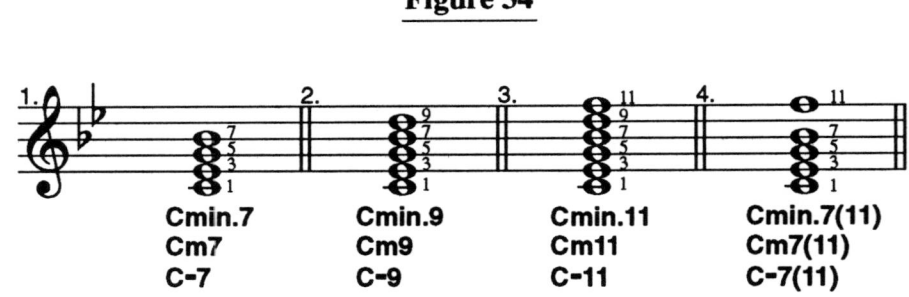

Content of the Minor 7th chords is as follows:

1.   C Min.7 contains the root, minor 3rd above the root, and perfect 5th above the root and minor 7th above the root.

2.   C Min.9 contains the root, minor 3rd, perfect 5th, minor 7th and major 9th.

3.   C Min.11 contains the root, minor 3rd, perfect 5th, minor 7th, major 9th and perfect 11th.

- 40 -

4. C Min.7(11) contains the root, minor 3rd, perfect 5th minor 7th and perfect 11th.

Note: Hereafter, the minor 3rd, the perfect 5th, the minor 7th, the major 9th and the perfect 11th will be referred to respectively as the 3rd, the 5th, the 7th, the 9th and the 11th when numerically indicating the content of a minor 7th chord.

D. Bass Voicings

A bass voicing consists of two notes. The bass voicings used when constructing a Minor 7th chord are as follows:

Figure 35

a. Root and 5th   b. Root and 7th

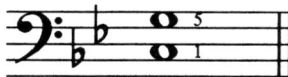   

c. Root and 10th   d. Optional - Root and 3rd

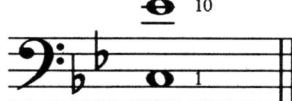   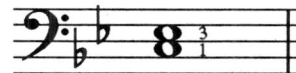

E. Rules for Voicing Minor 7th Chords

1. Use five notes when voicing a Minor 7th chord; no doubling of any tone is permitted.

2. The root, 3rd, and the 7th must be present in the Minor 7th chord; however, the 5th may be omitted if elected to do so.

3. Embellish the chord by using the added notes as indicated on p. 40.

4. Omit the 5th when the 9th and 11th are contained in the same chord voicing so as not to exceed a total of five (5) notes in the chord voiced.

5. To begin voicing Minor 7th chords, follow the method as illustrated in the "Amadiean Creed."

F. "Amadiean Creed": Method Used When Voicing Minor 7th Chords

The method used to voice Minor 7th chords is the "Amadiean Creed." The following examples, Figure 36 and Figure 37, illustrate the construction of C Minor 7th chord voicings by using the step by step application of the method. Realize that each note is numerically indicated throughout each of the four steps so as to point out the exact relationship of each note contained in the chord.

Voicing a Minor 7th chord using the Method (for example, C Minor 7).

Figure 36

"AMADIEAN CREED"

Step 1 (2 notes)

Select a bass voicing as illustrated in letter D. For example, the root and 7th.

Step 2 (add 1 note)

Put the 3rd in the chord if not present in the bass voicing.

Step 3 (add 2 notes)

Complete the chord voicing by choosing two notes from those available according to the rules in letter E; here they are the 5th, 9th, or the 11th. The notes chosen in Figure 36 are the 5th and the 9th.

Step 4 (Notation)

Notate the chord above the staff. Realize the chord results from applying the "Amadiean Creed," which is a system for voicing chords based on a 5-note model chord containing embellished tones with no doubling.

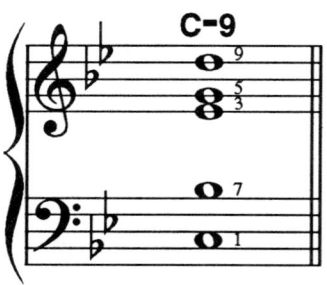

Figure 37 illustrates the voicing of a C Minor 7th chord using the "Amadiean Creed." However, note **Step 1**, when the 3rd has been selected in the bass voicing, or *indicated as the 10th*. For example, root and 3rd or root and 10th, the player needs to "adjust" **Step 2**. Furthermore, the adjustment of **Step 2**, as illustrated below, only occurs when the 3rd is selected in **Step 1**. Otherwise, **Step 2**, of the "Amadiean Creed", as outlined in Figure 36, is *never* adjusted.

<h2 style="text-align:center">Figure 37</h2>

"AMADIEAN CREED"

Step 1 (2 notes)

Select a bass voicing as illustrated in letter D. For example, the root and 10th.

Step 2 (add 1 note)

Put the 3rd in the chord. However when the 3rd is present in the bass voicing, "adjust" **Step 2** as follows: choose one note from the available notes which are derived from the rules in letter E; here they are the 5th, 7th, 9th or the 11th. Put the note chosen in one of the upper voices. For example, the note chosen in Figure 37 is the 7th.

Step 3 (add 2 notes)

Complete the chord voicing by choosing two notes from the remaining notes available. For example, the notes chosen in Figure 37 are the 9th and the 5th.

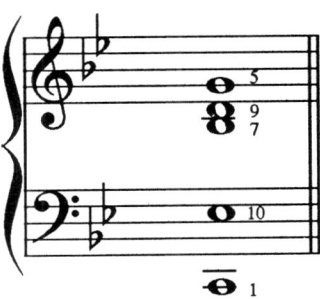

Step 4 (Notation)

Notate the chord above the staff. Realize the chord results from applying the "Amadiean Creed," which is a system for voicing chords based on a 5-note model chord containing embellished tones with no doubling.

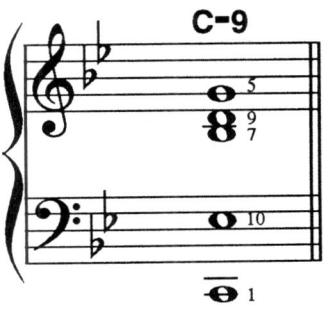

G. Examples of Minor 7th Chord Voicings

Figure 38

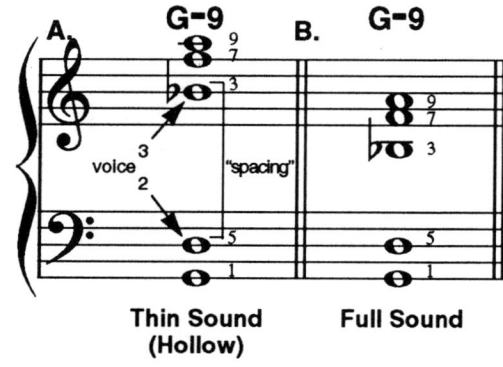

H. Rules Derived From Analysis: Spacing

"Spacing" (as mentioned in the previous Chapters 1 and 2) is the result of having too much distance between one voice and another within the chord, thus causing the chord to sound thin or hollow. To avoid spacing do not exceed an interval of a 7th between the 2nd and 3rd voice of the chord, also between the 3rd and 5th voice of the chord. For example, Figure 39A illustrates spacing between the 2nd voice "D" and the 3rd voice "Bb." The overall distance between these two voices is a -13th, the result of which produces a hollow sounding chord. However, in Figure 39B, spacing is avoided as a result of not exceeding an interval of a 7th between the second and third voice. Realize that by moving the top three voices down an octave, the content of the chord remains the same, but the sound of the chord is improved.

Figure 40A illustrates "spacing" between the 3rd voice "D" and the 5th voice "Eb." The overall distance between these two voices is a -9th, the result of which produces a hollow sounding chord. However, in Figure 40B spacing is avoided by not exceeding an interval of a 7th between the 3rd and 5th voice in the chord. Realize that by changing the position of the 3rd voice and the 5th voice in the chord, spacing is avoided and the sound of the chord is improved.

Figure 39

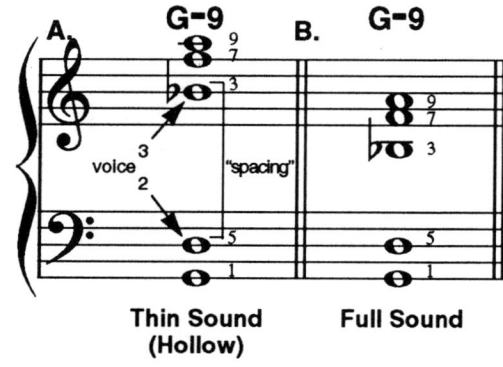

Figure 40

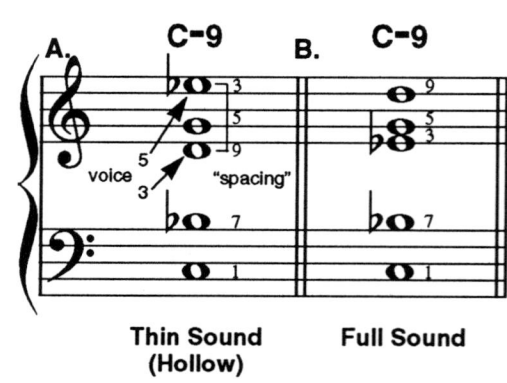

Now that the player has been given the background needed to construct Minor 7th chord voicings, the player is ready to apply the method. To clearly emphasize the method, the following EXERCISE I is limited to the C Minor 7th chords. However, the exercises that follow will cover all 12 Minor 7th chords.

I. ASSIGNMENT: CONSTRUCTING VOICINGS ON THE C MINOR 7TH CHORD

Using Measure 1 as a guide, construct Minor 7th chord voicings by applying the "Amadiean Creed." Each chord must contain the exact content as indicated in the notation, also indicate the content numerically. Upon completion of the exercise, refer to *Appendix I Chord Voicings, Chapter III, Exercise I.*

"AMADIEAN CREED"

EXERCISE I

Step 1 (2 notes)
Select a bass voicing as indicated in letter D.

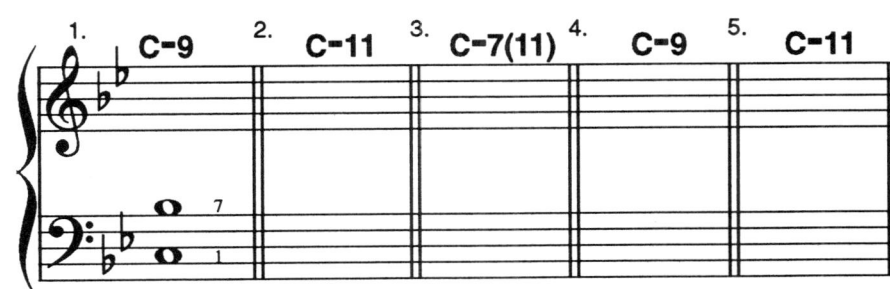

Step 2 (add 1 note)
Put the 3rd in the chord if not present in the bass voicing. However, if the 3rd is chosen in the bass voicing, see Figure 37 (Step 2).

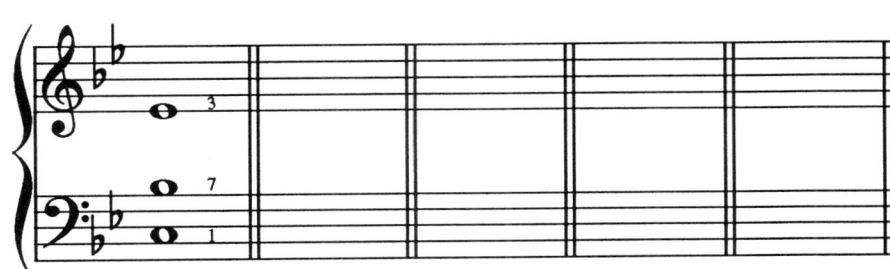

Step 3 (add 2 notes)
Complete the chord voicing as indicated in notation. Realize the two notes needed are derived from letter E, p.41. When completed, check for "spacing."

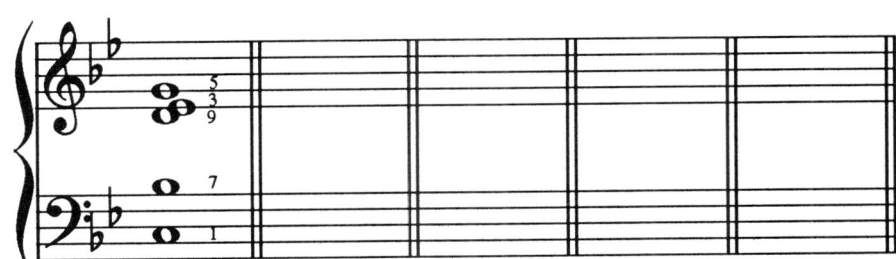

Step 4 (Notation)
Notate the chord above the staff. Realize the chord results from applying the "Amadiean Creed": a 5-note chord voicing with no doubling. Play the chord.

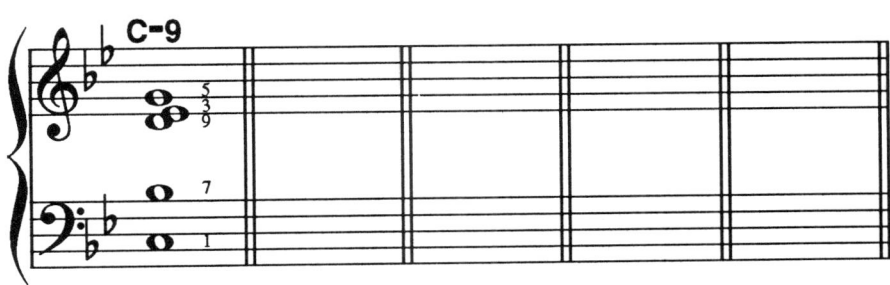

ASSIGNMENT: CONSTRUCTING VOICINGS ON THE MINOR 7TH CHORDS

Using the voicings of your choice, construct the following Minor 7th chords as indicated in the notation. Also indicate the content of each notated chord as illustrated in *measure 1*. See interpretation when reading "specific chord notation" Page 47, Letter A. Upon completion of the exercise, refer to *Appendix I Chord Voicings, Chapter III, Exercise II*.

EXERCISE II

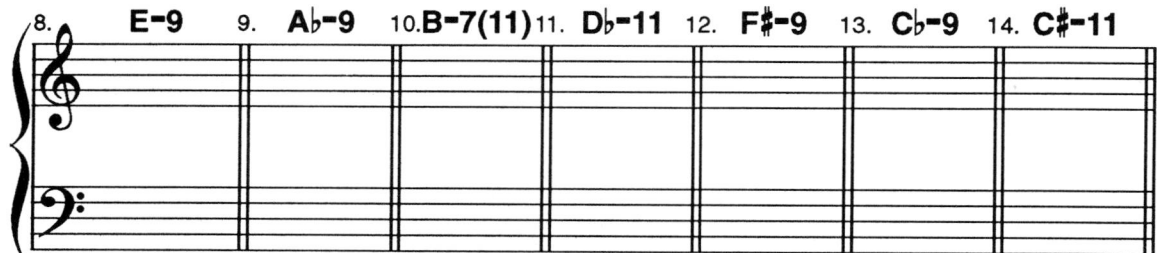

Refer to *Appendix I* as stated above before beginning the additional writing exercises.

For additional writing exercises: Construct 6 to 10 voicings of your choice using the embellished tones, according to the rules, on each of the following Minor 7th chords:

C-7, G-7, F-7, D-7, B♭-7, A-7, E♭-7, E-7, A♭-7, B-7, D♭-7, F♯-7, G♭-7, C♯-7, C♭-7.

It is suggested that each assignment should consist of approximately four Minor 7th chords.

PART II: INTERPRETATION AND PROCEDURE WHEN READING MINOR 7TH CHORD NOTATION

A.   Specific Chord Notation

    When reading specific chord notation of a Minor 7th chord, for example, as in EXERCISE II, Page 46, the player should use only the content of the specific chord as indicated.

B.   Basic Chord Notation

    When reading basic chord notation of a Minor 7th chord, for example, as in EXERCISE III, Page 48, the player is to embellish the basic chord by using the added notes as indicated on *Page 40, Letter B.*

C.   Procedure for Sightreading Chord Notation in Tempo - Applying the "Amadiean Creed"

1.   When sightreading chord notation, establish a slow tempo by counting a one measure rest.

2.   As you count the measure rest in tempo, think of Steps 1, 2 and 3 of the "Amadiean Creed." Continuing in tempo, play the voicings of your choice holding each chord for 4 beats throughout the exercise.

3.   When a mistake is made, Stop! Setting the tempo a little slower, count a one measure rest, allotting time to think of a voicing. Then voice the chord correctly in tempo.

D. Assignment: Sightreading Chord Notation

In Exercise III sightread the following Minor 7th chords using the added notes to embellish the basic notated chords. Follow the procedure for sightreading as indicated on *Page 47, Letter C.*

EXERCISE III

Play slowly

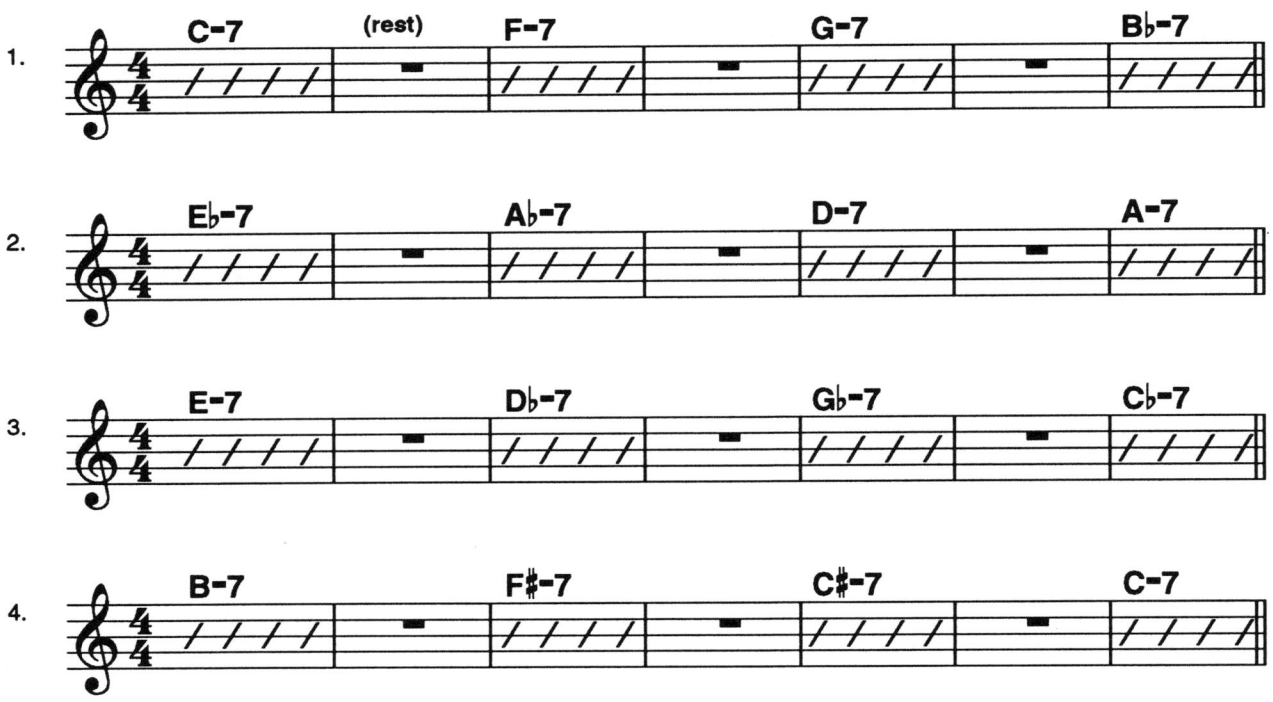

For additional sightreading exercises, read EXERCISE III in the following manner:

        1. RIGHT TO LEFT (◄—) each line;

        2. From TOP to BOTTOM (↓) each column; and

        3. From BOTTOM to TOP (↑) each column.

If a player feels insecure about any particular Minor 7th chords, he may, of course, formulate different series of Minor 7th chords to overcome his weakness by stressing the more difficult ones.

PART III: INTRODUCTION TO HARMONIZATION OF A MELODY USING MAJOR, MINOR AND MINOR 7TH CHORDS

Now that we have applied the method of constructing 5-note chord voicings to Minor 7th chords, we are ready to harmonize a melody using the Minor 7th chord. Also, in the examples that follow, melodies are harmonized utilizing the various types of chords learned thus far; namely, the Major, Minor and Minor 7th chords.

A. Background for Harmonization of a Melody: The "Harmonic Change"

As previously stated, when harmonizing a melody, the melody will be harmonized on the exact beat on which the "notated chords" occur indicated by the *left side* of the bracket (▼   ⌐). Also note that the bracket encloses all the notes contained within those beats that pertain to the same harmony. For example, in Figure 41A, measure 1: the CM9 occurs on the first beat above the note G; also realize that the following note "A" (enclosed in bracket) pertains to the CM9 harmony. Also in measure 1, the A-9 occurs on the third beat, above the note B, and the following notes B and C (enclosed in bracket) pertain to the A-9 harmony. In measure 2, the D-11 chord occurs on the first beat above the note G, and the following note "F" (enclosed in bracket) pertains to the D-11 harmony. Also in measure 2, the DbM9(6) occurs on the third beat above the note Bb, and the following note Ab (enclosed in bracket) pertains to the DbM9(6) harmony. In measure 3, the C6(9) occurs on the first beat above the note G and the bracket encloses all the beats that pertain to the C6(9) harmony. See Figures 41B and 41C for illustrations harmonizing the melody given in Figure 41A. Also note the analysis precedes the figure.

Figure 41A

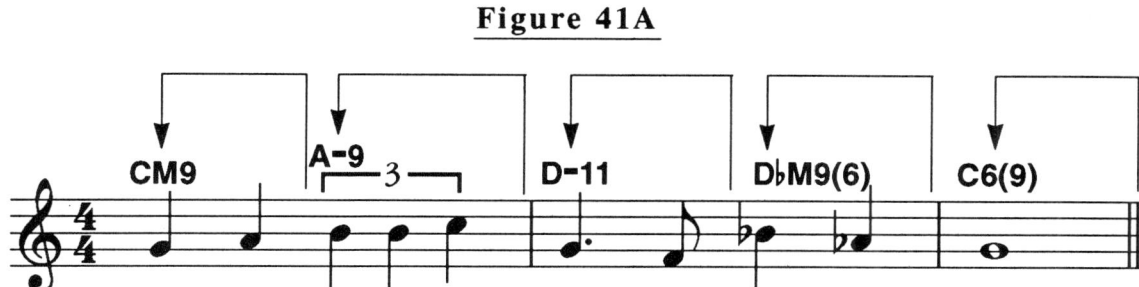

B. Analysis of the Procedure Used to Harmonize a Melody

Analysis of Figures 41B and 41C:

1. Each chord voicing occurs on the exact beat on which the chord is notated; (harmonic change) - indicated by (↓⎯⎯) left side of bracket.

2. The melody note appears in the top voice of the chord; also, the melody note that follows remains within the framework of that same harmony (enclosed in bracket) until the new harmonic change occurs.

3. Under the given melody note, at the point where the chord is notated, a bass voicing consisting of two notes was inserted in the bass, indicated by (⌉).

4. Two more tones indicated by (◄⎯⎯) were added to complete the 5-note chord voicing.

5. Realize that the notated chords in Figures 41B and 41C contain exactly the same notes; however, by changing the voicing of the same notated chord, realize the various sounds which are produced.

6. Realize that each chord voicing contains five (5) different notes and is a reflection of the material utilized in the "Amadiean Creed."

Figure 41B

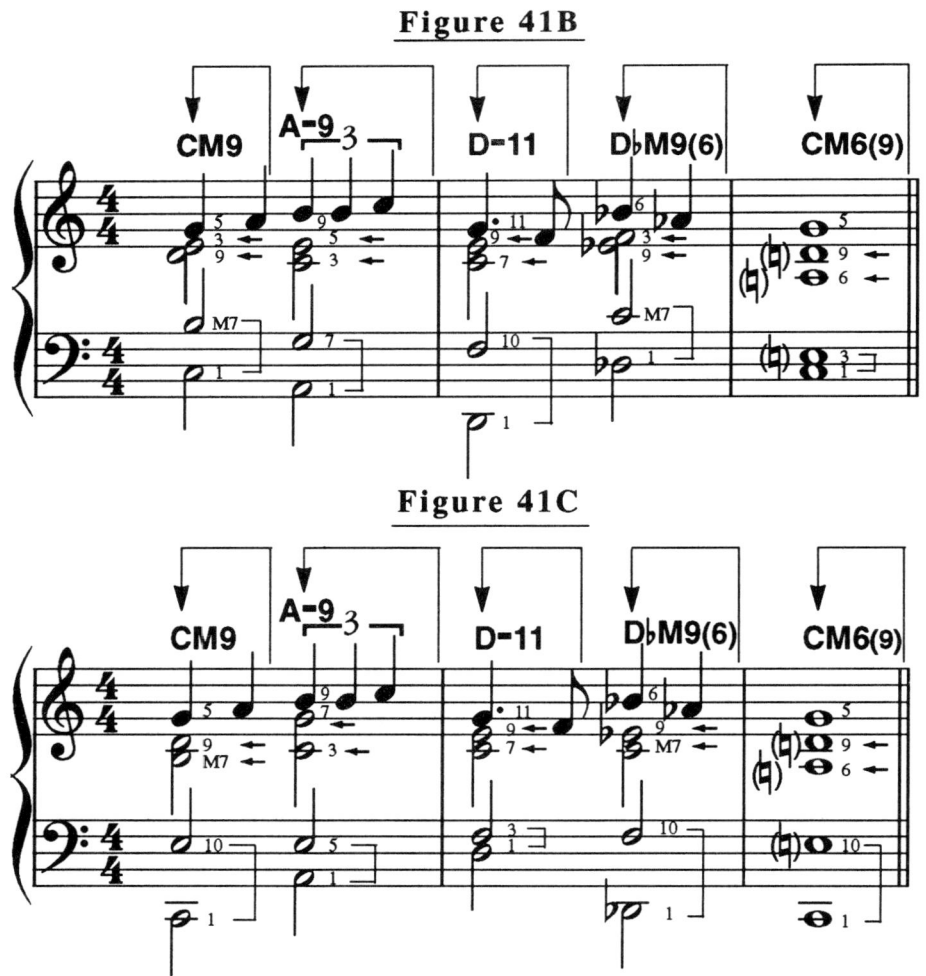

Figure 41C

C. Special Rules for Doubling Achieved through Specific Chord Voicings

When the root, 3rd, 5th or 7th is the melody note in a Minor 7th chord, that melody note can be doubled within the 5-note chord voicing. However, the doubling of tones is limited by utilizing specific chord voicings that best reflect the method.

Specific Chord Voicings

For example, when the root, 3rd, 5th or 7th is the melody note in a Minor 7th chord, that melody note can be doubled. In the examples that follow, the player should know each note contained in the specific chord voicings and then play those voicings in all keys. However, after learning the specific chord voicings as suggested, the player is free to experiment on his own and adjust his voicings according to his own personal taste. Note: "Spacing" is permitted only when the melody is doubled in the 3rd and 5th voice.
See Figures 43 and 45.

Figure 42

Root as the melody note;
Root doubled

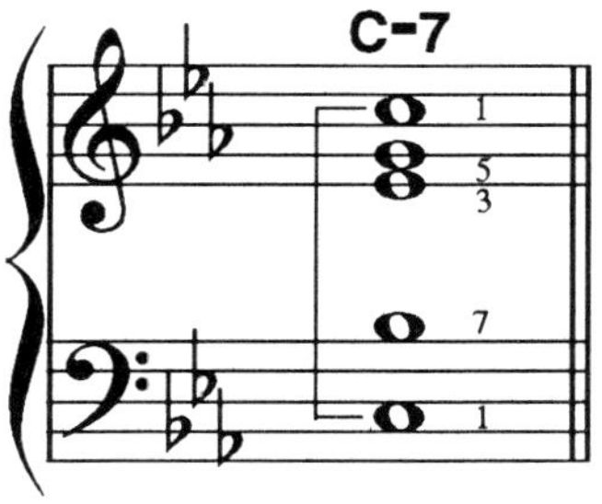

Figure 43

3rd as the melody note;
3rd doubled

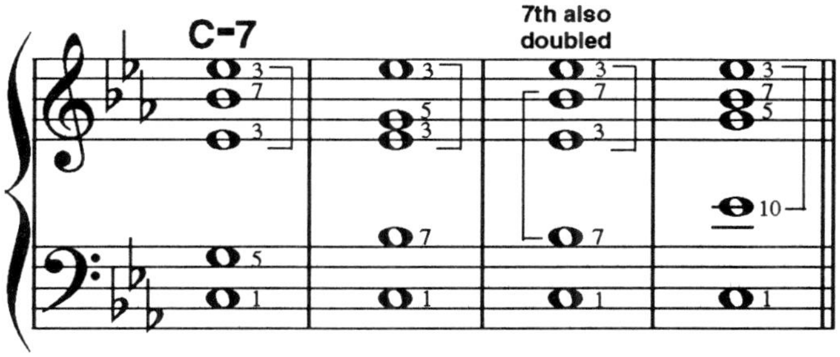

Figure 44

5th as the melody note;
5th doubled

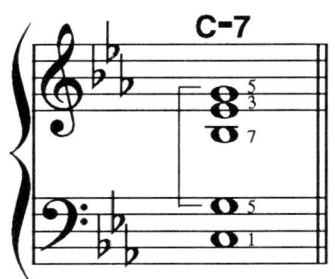

Figure 45

7th as the melody note;
7th doubled

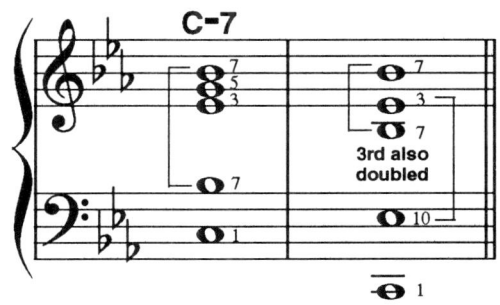

D. Utilizing Major, Minor and Minor 7th Chords

The following Figure 46A illustrates basic chords notated above melody notes to be harmonized. However, as mentioned on page 47, letter "B", the player is to embellish the basic notated chords. See Figure 46B, examples 1 and 2, for an illustration of harmonizing a melody embellishing the basic notated chords as given in Figure 46A. Also, note analysis precedes the figure.

Figure 46A

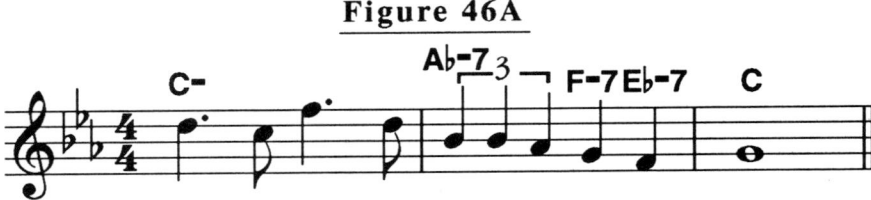

Analysis of a Harmonized Melody

Analysis of Figure 46B, examples 1 and 2:

1. Realize that when harmonizing a melody, the melody is harmonized on the exact beat on which the notated chord occurs by applying Steps 1 and 3 of the "method" in conjunction with #2 in letter E of the Rules for Voicing each type of chord discussed so far.

2. Realize that each of the basic notated chords, as given in Figure 46A, have been embellished throughout each example in Figure 46B.

3. Realize the different types of chords used throughout the examples; for instance, Major, Minor and Minor 7th chords.

4. Realize that each chord voicing is a reflection of the material utilized in the "Amadiean Creed."

Figure 46B

E. The "Flat 5" in the Minor 7th Chord

At times, a "flat 5" is notated in a minor 7th chord, usually when the flat 5 is the melody note. This indicates that the 5th degree of the basic minor 7th chord is lowered one-half step. The notation of a minor 7th chord containing a flat 5, for example, D F A♭ C is D-7(♭5). Note the following symbol (-) can also be used to denote the flat 5, for example (-5). However, for consistency we have chosen to use the symbol (♭5) throughout the text. See Figure 47.

Figure 47

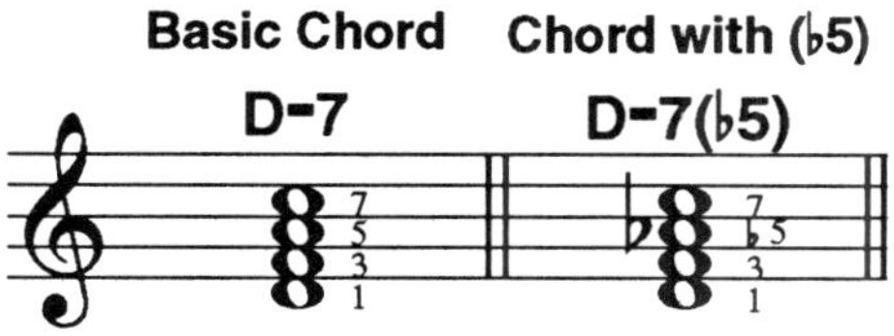

Basic Chord   Chord with (♭5)

As explained on p. 40, the minor 7th chord may be embellished by adding the 9th and the 11th. But in the case of a minor 7th chord containing a flat 5, avoid the 9th, because it conflicts with the harmony. But the 11th still may be used. On the other hand, in a situation involving the harmonization of a melody, and the flat 5 occurs as a melody note, double the flat 5 to complete the chord voicing.

F. Utilizing the "Flat 5" as the Melody Note

The following Figure 48A illustrates a melody line that contains the flat 5 as the melody note to be harmonized (see measures 1 and 3). See Figure 48B for an illustration harmonizing the flat 5 as the melody note. Also, note the analysis precedes the figure.

Figure 48A

Analysis of a Harmonized Melody

1.   Realize that the melody is harmonized on the exact beat on which the notated chord occurs.

2.   Realize that the basic notated chords, as given in Figure 48A, have been embellished in Figure 48B.

3.   Realize that the melody note is the flat 5 and is harmonized in measures 1 and 3.

4.   Realize that each voicing is a reflection of the material utilized in the "Amadiean Creed."

Figure 48B

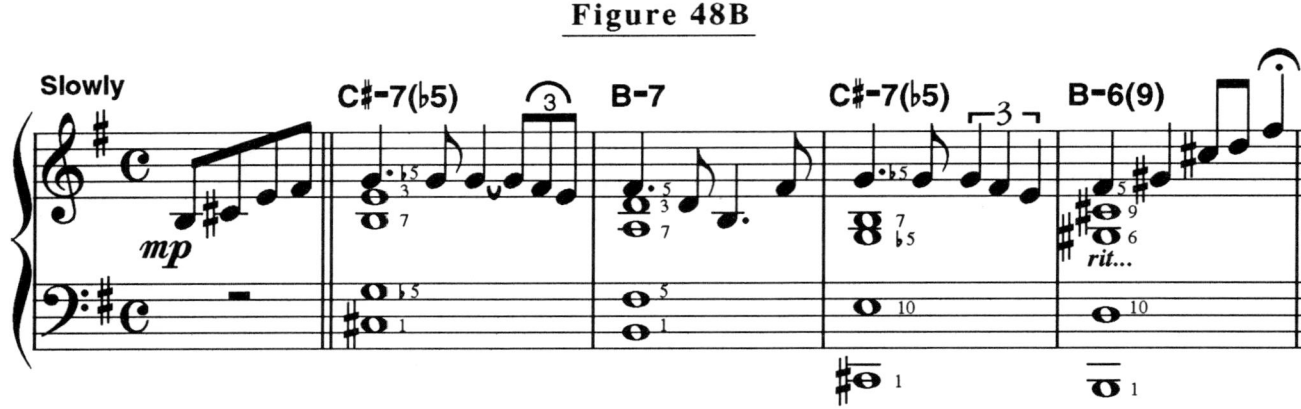

G.   Assignment: Harmonizing Melodies Using Major, Minor and Minor 7th Chords

Exercises 1 through 5

   In the following Exercises 1 through 5, the melody lines are specifically designed for the purpose of applying the "method" when harmonizing a melody using Major, Minor, and Minor 7th chords. Upon completion of the exercises, refer to *Appendix II Harmonized Melodies, Chapter III, Exercises 1 through 5.*

   Harmonize the melodies in the following exercises embellishing the basic notated chords. The embellished chords must be notated above the basic chord where indicated in notation. Also indicate the content of each chord numerically. For purposes of the exercises, play in a slow to moderate tempo.

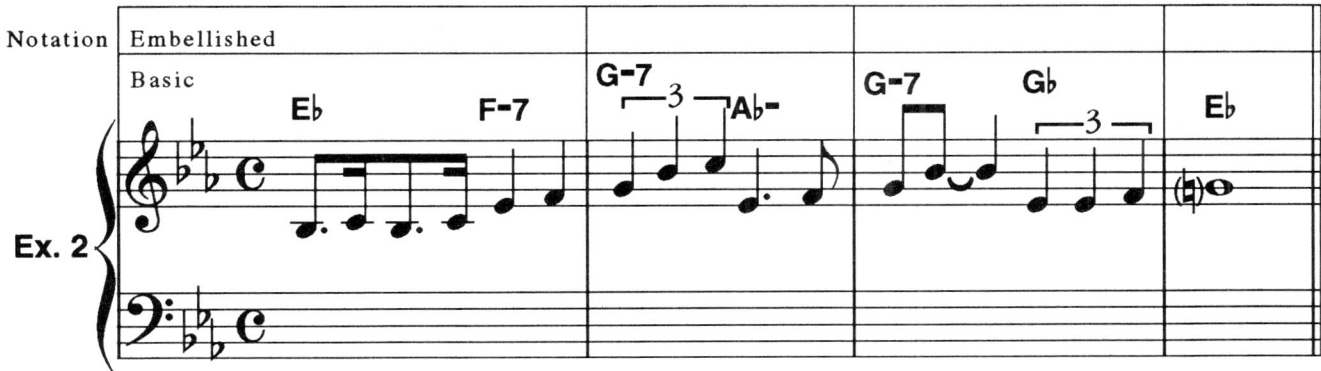

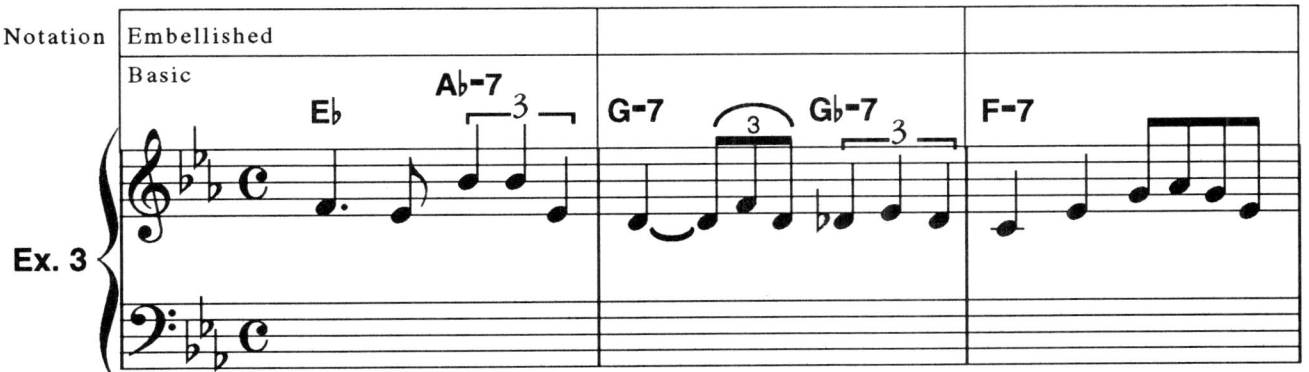

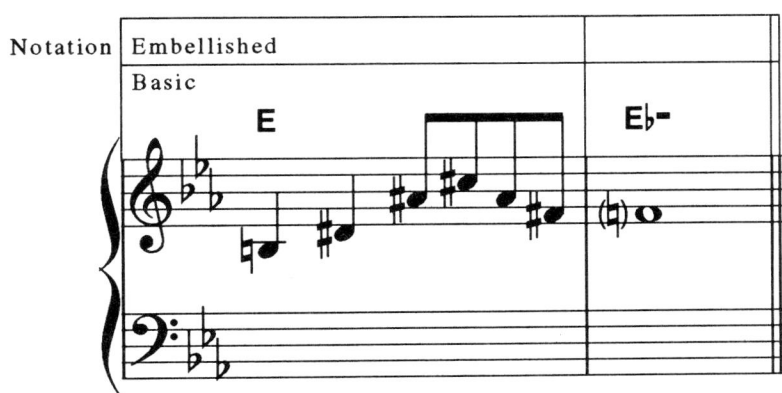

SUMMARY: CHAPTER III has given the player ample opportunity to utilize the concept of the method when harmonizing melodies using Major, Minor, and Minor 7th chords. However, our next chord, the Dominant 7th chord, when utilized with the previous types of chords, will bring into focus the full potential of the method as the melodies of original compositions are harmonized. Let us continue to progress by moving on to the next chord: the Dominant 7th chord.

CHAPTER IV - DOMINANT 7TH CHORDS

PART I: PREPARATION FOR VOICING DOMINANT 7TH CHORDS

A. Construction of Dominant 7th Chords

A dominant 7th chord may be constructed by superimposing three intervals, a major 3rd, a perfect 5th, and a minor 7th, above any note. The particular note chosen is termed the "root" of the chord.

Figure 49

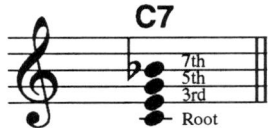

Also, a Dominant 7th chord can be constructed on the 5th degree of a major scale by combining that degree termed "root" (1) of the chord, and the following degrees located above that "root"; a 3rd, a 5th and 7th.

Figure 50

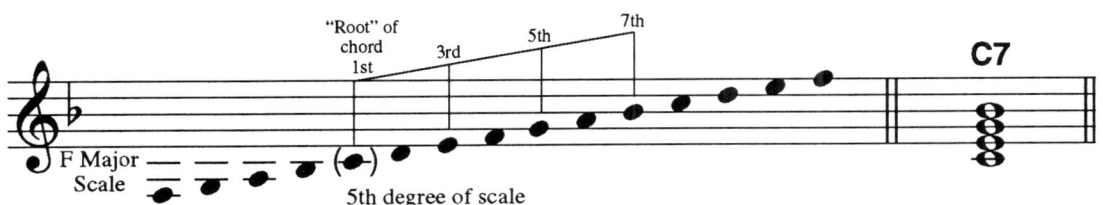

B. Embellishing a Dominant 7th Chord

Added Notes and Altered Notes

1. Added Notes

Added notes embellish the sound of a Dominant 7th chord. In popular music, standards, and jazz, when a Dominant 7th chord is indicated, it may be embellished by adding the following notes to the chord: the major 9th, the perfect 11th and the major 13th. These notes can be used individually or in combination with the Dominant 7th chord. Considering the root as 1st degree of the chord, the added notes are computed above that "root." For example, the major 9th - ninth step above the root; the perfect 11th - eleventh step above the root; the major 13th - thirteenth step above the root. Also, the suspended 4th (sus. 4) can be used to embellish the Dominant 7th chord. See explanation of the (sus. 4) at the conclusion of letter "C", Nos. 23, 24 and 25.

Figure 51

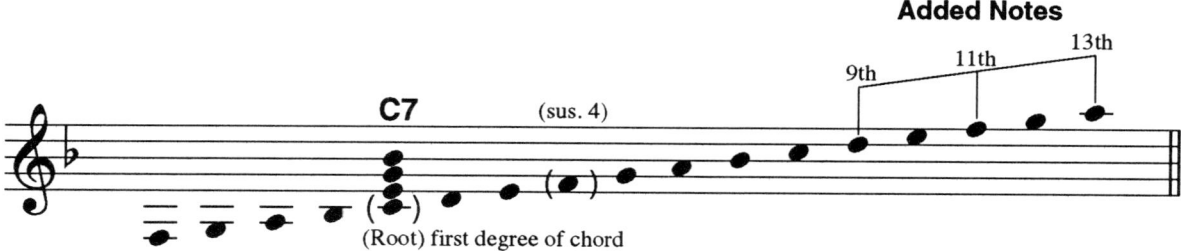

2. Altered Notes

When a Dominant 7th chord is indicated, the following altered notes may be added to the chord. For example, the flatted 5th (♭5), the flatted 5th step above the root; the augmented 5th (+5), the augmented 5th step above the root; the flatted 9th (♭9), the flatted 9th step above the root; the augmented 9th (+9), the augmented 9th step above the root; the augmented 11th (+11), the augmented 11th step above the root. Also, realize that the (♭5) and the (+11) are enharmonically the same tone.

Note: Various symbols can also be used to denote the altered 5th's and altered 9th's as illustrated in Figure 52; however, for consistency the flatted 5th and flatted 9th will be indicated (♭5) (♭9) and the augmented 5th and augmented 9th will be indicated (+5) (+9) in notation throughout the text. For example, see Figure 53.

Figure 52

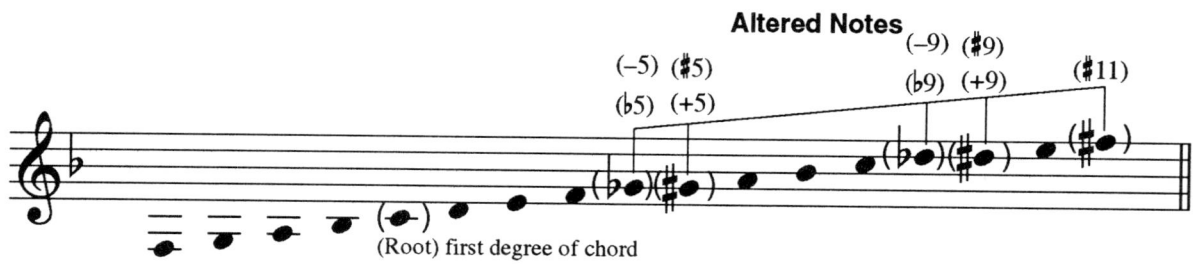

C. Notation of Dominant 7th Chords

Realize that the notation for Dominant 7th chords is "dom. 7". For example, C dom.7, C dom.9, C dom.11, etc. However, the notation given below is most often used; for example, C7, C9, C11, etc.

Figure 53

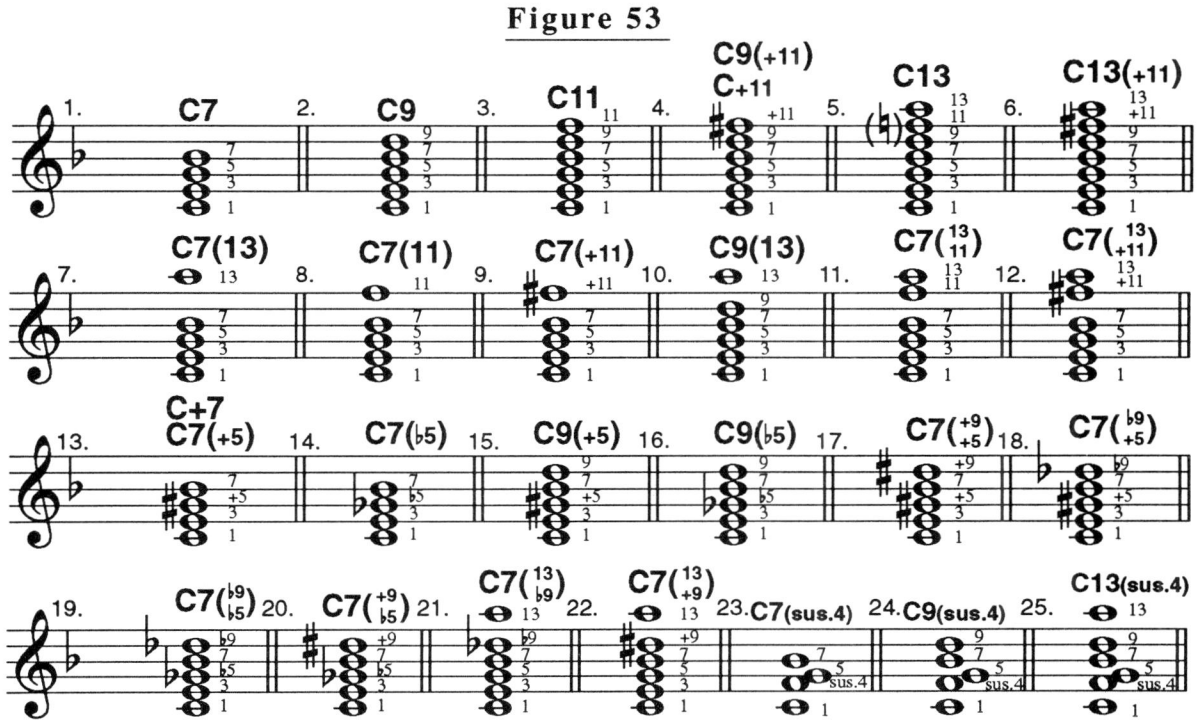

Content of the various Dominant 7th chords is as follows:

1. C7 contains the root, major 3rd above the root, perfect 5th above the root, and minor 7th above the root.

2. C9 contains the root, the major 3rd, the perfect 5th, the minor 7th, and the major 9th.

3. C11 contains the root, major 3rd, perfect 5th, minor 7th, major 9th, and the perfect 11th.

4. C+11 contains the root, major 3rd, perfect 5th, minor 7th, major 9th, and augmented 11th. Also notated C9(+11).

5. C13 contains the root, major 3rd, perfect 5th, minor 7th, major 9th, perfect 11th, and major 13th.

6. C13(+11) contains the root, major 3rd, perfect 5th, minor 7th, major 9th, augmented 11th, and major 13th.

7. C7(13) contains the root, major 3rd, perfect 5th, minor 7th, and major 13th.

8. C7(11) contains the root, major 3rd, perfect 5th, minor 7th, and perfect 11th.

9. C7(+11) contains the root, major 3rd, perfect 5th, minor 7th, and augmented 11th.

10. C9(13) contains the root, major 3rd, perfect 5th, minor 7th, major 9th, and major 13th.

11. $C7(^{13}_{11})$ contains the root, major 3rd, perfect 5th, minor 7th, perfect 11th, and major 13th.

12. $C7(^{13}_{+11})$ contains the root, major 3rd, perfect 5th, minor 7th, augmented 11th, and major 13th.

13. C7(+5) contains the root, major 3rd, augmented 5th, and minor 7th. Also notated C+7.

14. C7(♭5) contains the root, major 3rd, flatted 5th, and minor 7th.

15. C9(+5) contains the root, major 3rd, augmented 5th, minor 7th, and major 9th.

16. C9(♭5) contains the root, major 3rd, flatted 5th, minor 7th, and major 9th.

17. $C7(^{+9}_{+5})$ contains the root, major 3rd, augmented 5th, minor 7th, and augmented 9th.

18. $C7(^{♭9}_{+5})$ contains the root, major 3rd, augmented 5th, minor 7th, and flatted 9th.

19. $C7(^{♭9}_{♭5})$ contains the root, major 3rd, flatted 5th, minor 7th, and flatted 9th.

20. $C7(^{+9}_{♭5})$ contains the root, major 3rd, flatted 5th, minor 7th, and augmented 9th.

21. $C7(^{13}_{♭9})$ contains the root, major 3rd, perfect 5th, minor 7th, flatted 9th, and major 13th.

22. $C7(^{13}_{+9})$ contains the root, major 3rd, perfect 5th, minor 7th, augmented 9th, and major 13th.

23. C7(sus.4) contains the root, perfect 4th, perfect 5th, and minor 7th. The distinctive quality of this chord is the result of inserting the perfect 4th and omitting the major 3rd.

24. C9(sus.4) contains the root, perfect 4th, perfect 5th, minor 7th and major 9th.

25. C13(sus.4) contains the root, perfect 4th, perfect 5th, minor 7th, major 9th, and major 13th.

   Note: When a (sus.4) is indicated in a dominant 7th chord, the 3rd must be omitted.

   Note: Hereafter, the major 9th, perfect 11th and the major 13th will be referred to respectively as the 9th, the 11th and the 13th when numerically indicating the content of a dominant 7th chord.

D. Bass Voicings

A bass voicing consists of two notes. The bass voicing used when constructing a Dominant 7th chord are as follows:

Figure 54

a. Root and 5th

b. Root and 7th

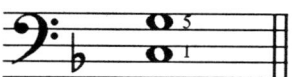
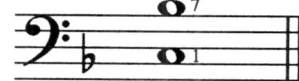

c. Root and 10th

d. Optional - Root and 3rd

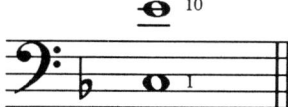

E. Rules for Voicing Dominant 7th Chords

1. Use five (5) different notes when voicing a Dominant 7th chord; no doubling of any note is permitted.

2. The root, 3rd and 7th must be present in the Dominant 7th chord; however, the 5th can be omitted if elected to do so.

3. Embellish the chord by using the added notes and/or alteres notes indicated on page 58, letter "B," 1 and 2. However, do not exceed a total of five (5) notes in the chord voiced.

4. When using the suspended 4th (sus.4) in a Dominant 7th chord, the 3rd must be omitted. Also in this chord, avoid using the altered notes, as these notes tend to detract from the character of the chord. However, the *added* notes can be used without detracting from the chord.

5. To begin voicing Dominant 7th chords, follow the method as illustrated in the "Amadiean Creed."

F. "Amadiean Creed": Method Used When Voicing Dominant 7th Chords

The method used to voice Dominant 7th chords is the "Amadiean Creed." The following examples, Figure 55A and Figure 56A, illustrate the construction of C7 chord voicings using the step-by-step application of the method. In addition, due to the dominating factor of the Dominant 7th chord, the resolution of this chord, built on the 5th degree of the scale, resolves to the tonic (1st degree) of that scale. For example, the C7 chord resolves to the F chord. Therefore, upon completion of each Figure, 55A and 56A, the following Figures, 55B and 56B, will illustrate the resolution of each Dominant 7th chord to the tonic. These illustrations will serve to benefit the player in a number of ways. For example: 1) it will demonstrate one of the basic functions of the Dominant 7th chord, that which resolves to the Tonic chord; and, 2) it will give the player the opportunity to hear the voicings, as a result of the method, in the context of a completed musical idea. Realize that each note is numerically indicated throughout each of the four steps so as to point out the exact relationship contained in the chord.

Voicing a Dominant 7th chord using the Method (for example, C Dominant 7th).

Figure 55A

"AMADIEAN CREED"

Step 1 (2 notes)

Select a bass voicing as illustrated in letter D. For example, the root and 7th.

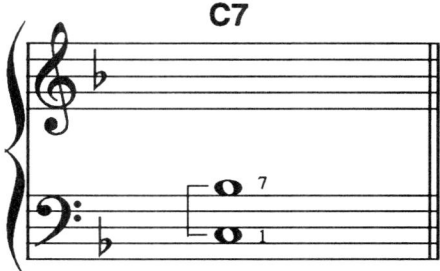

Step 2 (add 1 note)

Put the 3rd in the chord if not present in the bass voicing.

Step 3 (add 2 notes)

Complete the chord voicing by choosing two notes from those available according to the rules in letter E; here they are the 5, +5, ♭5, 7, 9, +9, +11, ♭9 or the 13th. The notes chosen in Figure 55A are the +9 and the +5. (Note that for simplicity, the suspended 4th is not dealt with here; it will be treated on p. 68.)

Step 4 (Notation)

Notate the chord above the staff. Realize the chord results from applying the "Amadiean Creed," which is a system for voicing chords based on a 5-note model chord containing embellished tones with no doubling.

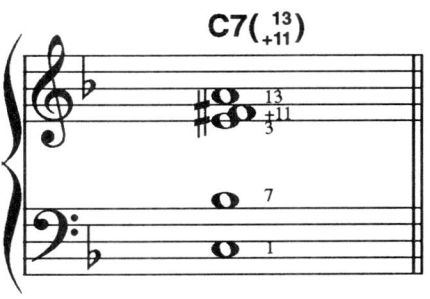

Figure 55B

The following Figure 55B illustrates one of the basic functions of a Dominant 7th chord: resolving to the tonic. For example, $C7(^{13}_{+11})$ to FM9. Play the chord.

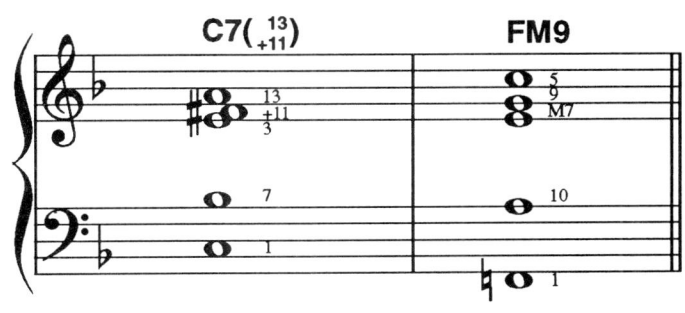

Figure 56A illustrates the voicing of a C Dominant 7th chord using the "Amadiean Creed." However, note *Step 1*, when the 3rd has been selected in the bass voicing, or *indicated as the 10th*. For example, root and 3rd or root and 10th, the player needs to "adjust" *Step 2*. Furthermore, the adjustment of *Step 2*, as illustrated below, only occurs when the 3rd is selected in *Step 1*. Otherwise, *Step 2* of the "Amadiean Creed," as outlined in Figure 55A is *never* adjusted.

Figure 56A

"AMADIEAN CREED"

Step 1 (2 notes)

Select a bass voicing as illustrated in letter D. For example, the root and 10th.

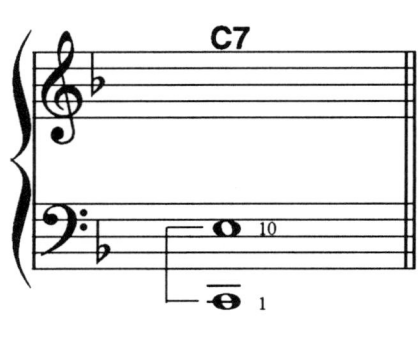

Step 2 (add 1 note)

Put the 3rd in the chord. However, when the 3rd is present in the bass voicing, "adjust" *Step 2* as follows: choose one note from the available notes which are derived from the rules in letter E; here they are the 5, +5, ♭5, 7, 9, +9, ♭9, +11 or the 13th. Put the note chosen in one of the upper voices. For example, the note chosen in Figure 56A is the 7th.

Step 3 (add 2 notes)

Complete the chord voicing by choosing two notes from the remaining notes available, for example, the notes chosen in Figure 56A are the +9 and the +5.

Step 4 (Notation)

Notate the chord above the staff. Realize the chord results from applying the "Amadiean Creed," which is a system for voicing chords based on a 5-note model chord with embellished tones and without doubling.

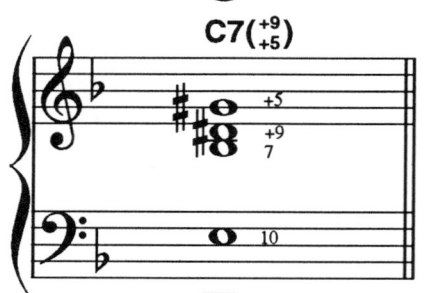

The following Figure 56B illustrates one of the basic functions of a Dominant 7th chord: resolving to the tonic. For example, C7($^{+9}_{+5}$) to FM9(6). Play each chord.

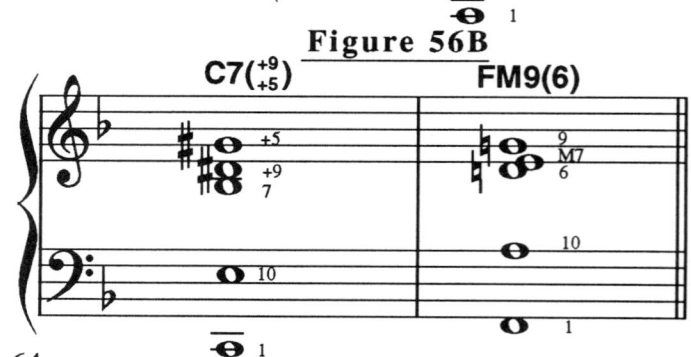

Figure 56B

- 64 -

G. Examples of Dominant 7th Chord Voicings Resolving to Major Chord Voicings

The resolution of the Dominant 7th chord to the tonic chord is an example of a complete musical idea utilizing the application of the method. However, it is important to realize that in resolving the Dominant 7th chord to the tonic as given below, there is no specific *tonic* chord voicing implied in any example to be the best or only voicing possible. As the player becomes familiar with Dominant 7th chords, there will be ample opportunity to resolve a specific Dominant 7th voicing to various voicings of the tonic. This will afford the player the opportunity to develop his own taste accordingly.

Figure 57

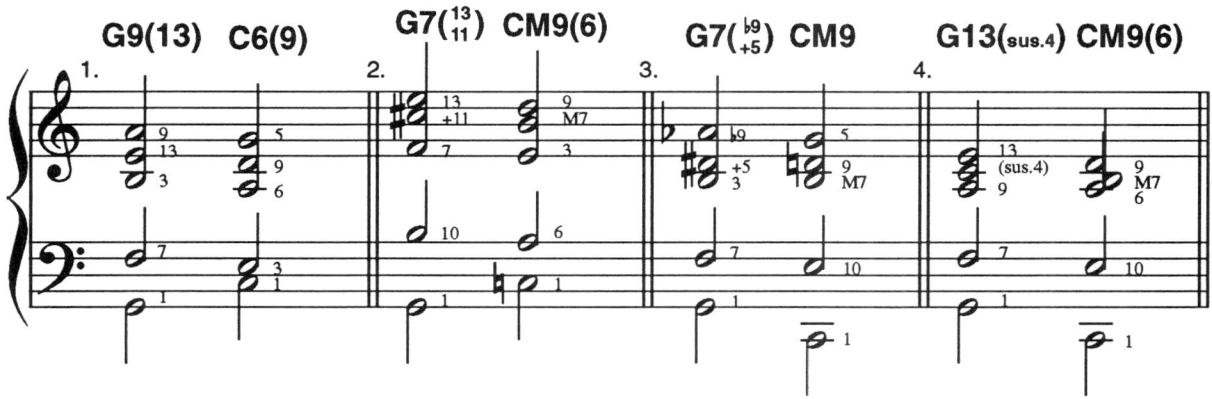

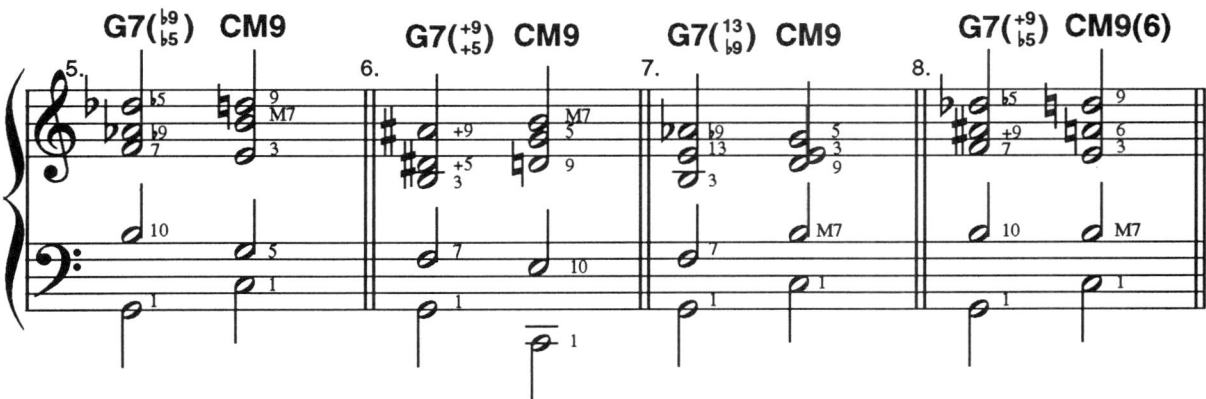

The following Figure 58 and Figure 59 are examples illustrating a specific voicing of a Dominant 7th chord resolving to various voicings of the Tonic. The player should realize that even though notes in the Dominant 7th chord tend to resolve to certain notes in the Tonic chord, it is not the intention of the author to limit the player only to these resolutions, but rather to encourage him to experiment with specific voicings of Dominant 7th chords resolving to various voicings of the Tonic chord, as illustrated in Figures 58 and 59.

Figure 58

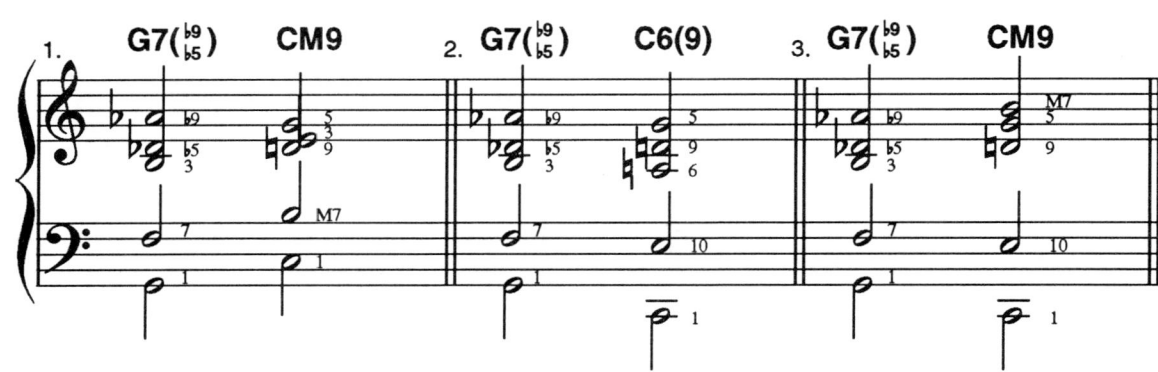

Figure 59

H. Rules Derived from Analysis: Spacing

"Spacing" (as mentioned in the previous chapters) is the result of having too much distance between one voice and another within the chord, thus causing the chord to sound thin or hollow. To avoid spacing in the Dominant 7th chord, do not exceed an interval of a 7th between the 2nd and 3rd voice in the chord or between the 3rd and 5th voice in the chord. For example, Figure 60A illustrates spacing between the second voice "F" and the third voice "B". The overall distance between the two voices is an augmented 11th, the result of which produces a hollow sounding chord. However, in Figure 60B, spacing is avoided as a result of not exceeding an interval of a 7th between the second and third voice. Realize that by moving the top three voices down an octave, the content of the chord remains the same, but the sound of the chord is improved.

Figure 61A illustrates spacing between the third voice "E" and the fifth voice "F#." The overall distance between these two voices is a 9th, the result of which produces a hollow sounding chord. However, in Figure 61B, spacing is avoided by not exceeding an interval of a 7th between the third and fifth voice within the chord. Realize that by changing the position of the third voice and the fifth voice in the chord, spacing is avoided and the sound of the chord is improved.

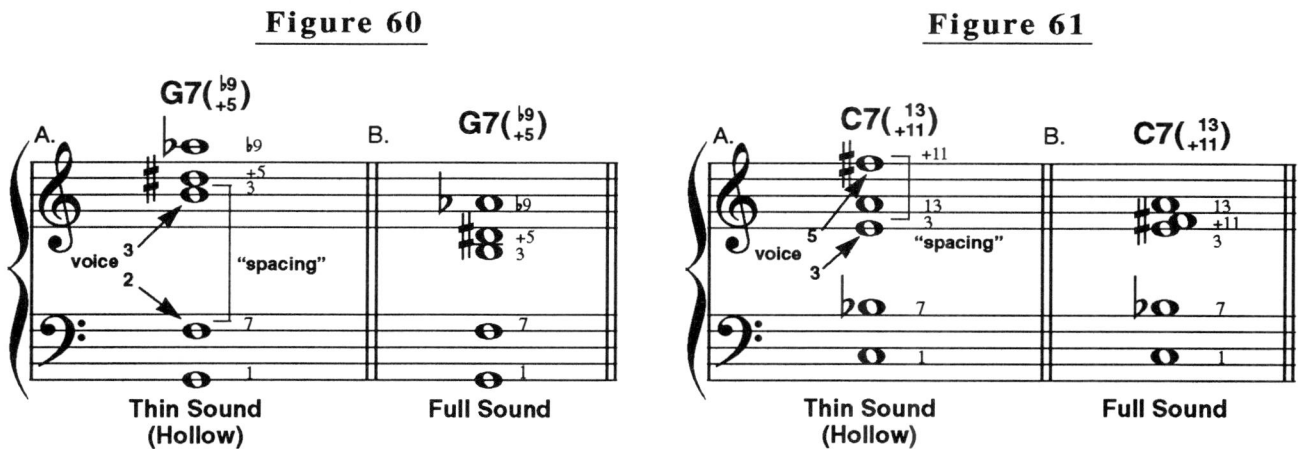

Figure 60   Figure 61

Now that the player has been given the background needed to construct Dominant 7th chord voicings, the player is ready to apply the method. To clearly emphasize the principle of the method, the following Exercise I is limited to the C Dominant 7th chords. However, the exercises that follow will cover all 12 Dominant 7th chords.

I.   ASSIGNMENT: CONSTRUCTING VOICINGS ON THE C DOMINANT 7TH CHORD

Using measure 1 as a guide, construct Dominant 7th chord voicings by applying the "Amadiean Creed." Each chord must contain the exact content as indicated in the notation, also indicate the content numerically. Notice the (sus.4) indicated in the Dominant 7th chord in No. 3. When this occurs, *adjust step 2 of the method* as follows: Omit the 3rd and insert the (sus.4) in Step 2 of the method as illustrated below. Upon completion of the exercise, refer to *Appendix I Chord Voicings, Chapter IV, Exercise I.*

EXERCISE I

"AMADIEAN CREED"

Step 1 (2 notes)

Select a bass voicing as indicated in letter D.

Step 2 (add 1 note)

Put the 3rd in the chord if not present in the bass voicing. However, if the 3rd is chosen in the bass voicing, see *Figure 56A* (Step 2).

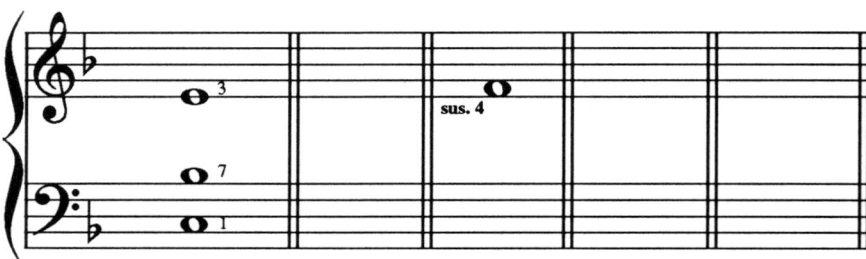

Step 3 (add 2 notes)

Complete the chord voicing as indicated in notation. Realize the two notes needed are derived from letter E, p. 61. When completed, check for "spacing."

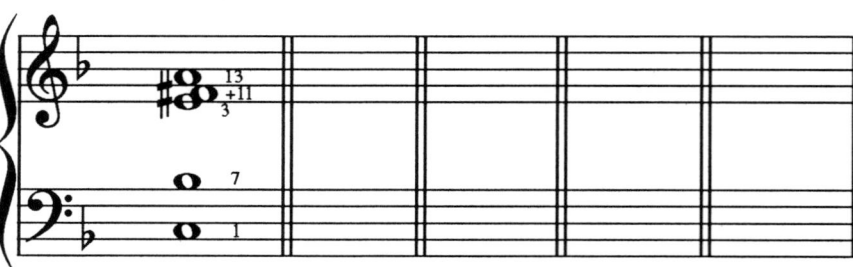

Step 4 (Notation)

Notate the chord above the staff. Realize the chord results from applying the "Amadiean Creed": a 5-note chord voicing with no doubling. Play the chord.

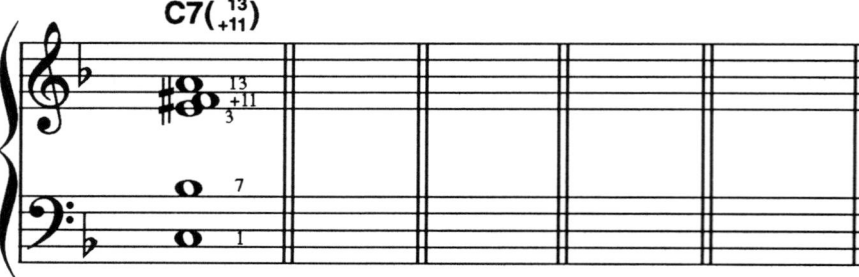

ASSIGNMENT: CONSTRUCTING VOICINGS ON THE REMAINING DOMINANT 7TH CHORDS

Using the voicings of your choice, construct the following Dominant 7th chords resolving to the Major chords as indicated in the notation. Also indicate the content of each chord as illustrated in *measure 1*. See interpretation when reading "specific chord notation" Page 70, Letter A. Upon completion of the exercise, refer to *Appendix I Chord Voicings, Chapter IV, Exercise II.*

EXERCISE II

Refer to *Appendix I* as stated above before beginning the additional writing exercises.

For additional writing exercises: Construct 6 to 10 voicings of your choice using the embellished tones, according to the rules, on each of the following Dominant 7th chords resolving to the Major chords:

C7 to F, G7 to C, F7 to B♭, D7 to G, B♭7 to E♭, A7 to D, E♭7 to A♭, E7 to A, A♭7 to D♭,

B7 to E, D♭7 to G♭, F♯7 to B, G♭7 to C♭, C♯7 to F♯, C♭7 to F♭ or E.

It is suggested that each assignment should consist of approximately four Dominant 7th chords resolving to four Major chords.

PART II: INTERPRETATION AND PROCEDURE WHEN READING DOMINANT 7TH CHORD NOTATION

A. Specific Chord Notation

When reading specific chord notation of Dominant 7th chords, for example, as in EXERCISE II, Page 69, the player should use only the content of the specific chord as indicated.

B. Basic Chord Notation

When reading basic chord notation of Dominant 7th chords, for example, as in EXERCISE III, Page 71, the player is to embellish the basic chord by using the added and altered notes as indicated on *Page 58, Letter B*.

C. Procedure for Sightreading Chord Notation in Tempo - Applying the "Amadiean Creed"

1. When sightreading chord notation, establish a slow tempo by counting a one measure rest.

2. As you count the measure rest in tempo, think of Steps 1, 2, and 3 of the "Amadiean Creed." Continuing in tempo, play the voicings of your choice holding each chord for 4 beats throughout the exercise.

3. When a mistake is made, Stop! Setting the tempo a little slower, count a one measure rest, allotting time to think of a voicing. Then voice the chord correctly in tempo.

D. Assignment: Sightreading Chord Notation

In Exercise III, sightread the following Dominant 7th chords using the altered and added notes to embellish the basic notated Dominant 7th chords. Follow the procedure for sightreading as indicated on *Page 70, Letter C*.

EXERCISE III

Play slowly

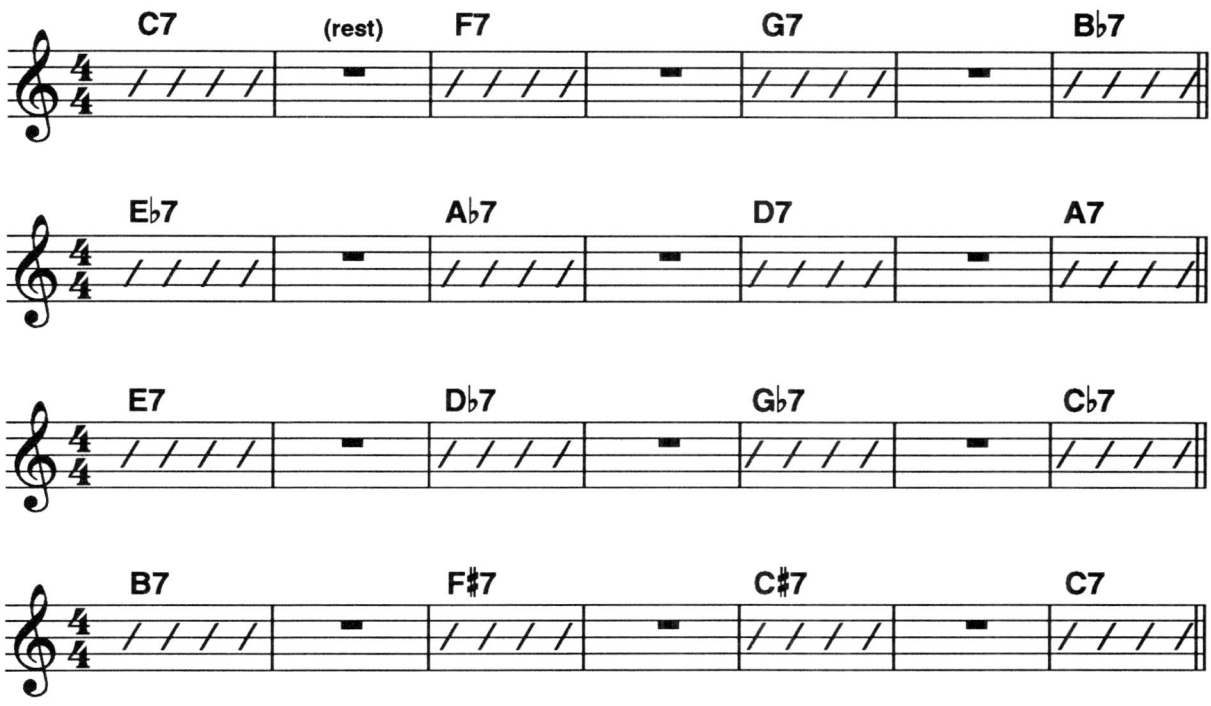

For additional sightreading exercises, read EXERCISE III in the following manner:

1. RIGHT TO LEFT (◄──) each line;
2. From TOP to BOTTOM (↓) each column; and
3. From BOTTOM to TOP (↑) each column.

If a player feels insecure about any particular Dominant 7th chords, he may, of course, formulate different series of Dominant 7th chords to overcome his weakness by stressing the more difficult ones.

PART III: INTRODUCTION TO HARMONIZATION OF A MELODY USING MAJOR, MINOR, MINOR 7TH AND DOMINANT 7TH CHORDS

Now that we have applied the method of constructing 5-note chord voicings to Dominant 7th chords, we are ready to harmonize a melody using the Dominant 7th chord. Also, in the examples that follow, melodies are harmonized using the various types of chords learned thus far; namely, Major, Minor, Minor 7th and Dominant 7th chords.

A. Background for Harmonization of a Melody: The "Harmonic Change"

As previously stated, when harmonizing a melody, the melody note will be harmonized on the exact beat on which the notated chord occurs. In addition, when chords are notated above a rest (𝄽), this indicates that there is no melody note to be harmonized; however, the notated chord must be voiced on the exact beat on which the rest occurs, indicated by the *left side* of the bracket (▼▔▔). Also note that the bracket encloses all notes contained within those beats that pertain to the same harmony. For example, in Figure 62A, measure 1: the FM9 occurs on the first beat above the note "C"; also the following note "D" (enclosed in bracket) pertains to the FM9 harmony. Also in measure 1, the D-9 occurs on the third beat above the note "A", and the bracket encloses all the beats that pertain to the D-9 harmony. In measure 2, the G-9 occurs on the first beat above the rest and the following notes "G" and "A" (enclosed in bracket) pertain to the G-9 harmony. Also in measure 2, the A7($^{13}_{\flat 9}$) occurs on the third beat above the note "B♭" and the following note "C" (enclosed in bracket) pertains to the A7($^{13}_{\flat 9}$) harmony. Finally, the C7($^{13}_{\flat 9}$) occurs on the fourth beat above the note "D♭" and the following note "D♯" (enclosed in bracket) pertains to the C7($^{13}_{\flat 9}$) harmony. In measure 3, the FM9 chord occurs on the first beat above the note "C" and the bracket encloses all the beats that pertain to the FM9 harmony. See Figure 62B for an illustration of harmonizing the melody given in 62A. Also note the analysis precedes the figure.

Figure 62A

B. Analysis of the Procedure Used to Harmonize a Melody

Analysis of Figure 62B:

1. Each chord voicing occurs on the exact beat on which the chord is notated, (harmonic change) indicated by (↓▭) left side of bracket.

2. The melody note appears in the top voice of the chord; also, the melody notes that follow remain within the framework of that same harmony (enclosed in bracket) until the new harmonic change occurs.

3. Under the given melody note, at the point where the chord is notated, a bass voicing consisting of two notes is inserted in the bass, indicated by (⌐).

4. Two more notes, indicated by (◀▬) are added to complete the 5-note chord voicing.

5. Realize that when a chord is notated above a rest (𝄽), the notated chord must be voiced on the exact beat on which the rest occurs. See measure 2. Notice that in the absence of a melody note here, three notes are added to complete the chord.

6. Realize that each chord voicing contains five (5) different notes and is a reflection of the material utilized in the "Amadiean Creed."

Figure 62B

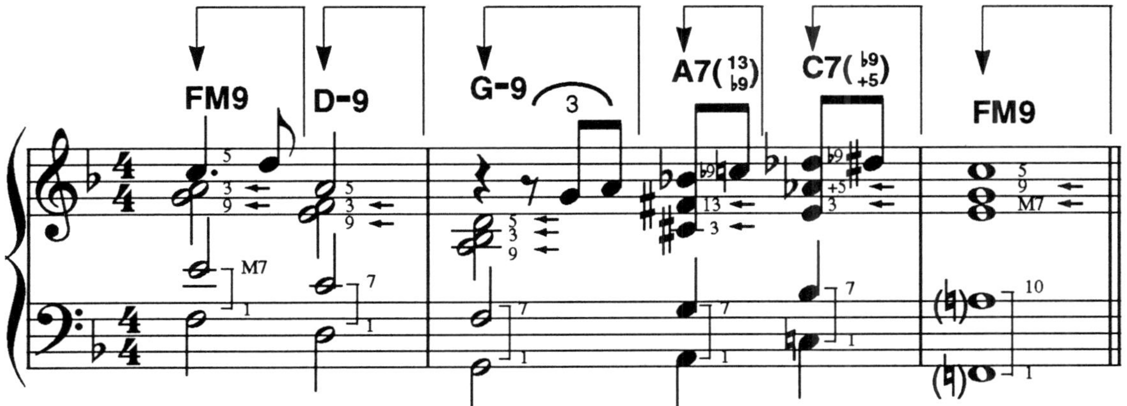

C. Special Rules for Doubling Achieved through Specific Chord Voicings

When the root or 3rd of the Dominant 7th chord is the melody note, that melody note can be doubled within the 5-note chord voicing. However, the doubling of tones is limited by utilizing specific chord voicings that best reflect the method.

Specific Chord Voicings

For example, when the root or the 3rd is the melody note in a Dominant 7th chord, that melody note can be doubled. In the examples that follow, the player should know each note in the specific chord voicings and then play those voicings in all keys. However, after learning the specific chord voicings as suggested, the player is free to experiment on his own and adjust his voicings according to his own personal taste. Note: "Spacing" is permitted only when the melody is doubled in the 3rd and 5th voice. See Figure 64.

Figure 63

Root as the melody note;
melody note doubled.

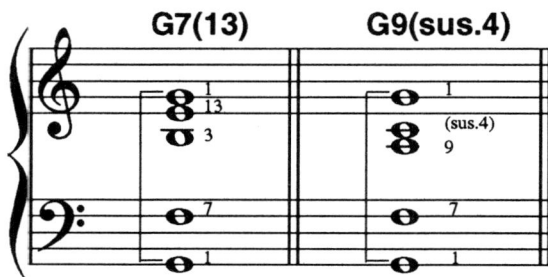

Figure 64

3rd as the melody note;
melody note doubled.

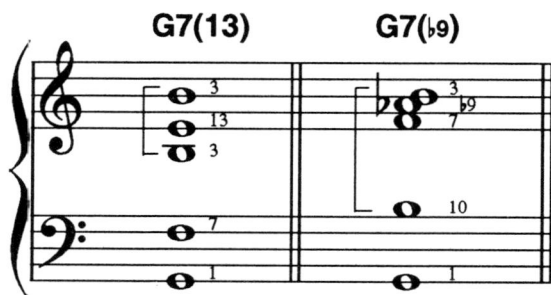

D. Optional Four-Note Chord

A four (4) note chord voicing is constructed and governed by the same rules applied to constructing five (5) note chord voicings as outlined in the "Amadiean Creed." The only difference is that the optional chord contains a total of four notes and not five. Therefore, when voicing a four (4) note chord, adjust Step 3 of the method as follows: complete the chord voicing by choosing one note according to the Rules for Voicing in letter E of each type of chord.

The function of the optional 4-note chord is *one of necessity* and also *one of choice.* For instance:

1. *It is of necessity,* when harmonizing a melody note that is in the low-middle register of the piano, approximately around "G" below middle "C" to the "E" above. For example, at times voicing a 5-note chord in this area of the keyboard may tend to produce a heavy or distorted sounding chord. However, voicing a 4-note chord in the low-middle register of the piano is totally effective and desirable. For examples illustrating the optional 4-note chord see Figure 65B, following the analysis in letter "E".

2. *It is of necessity* also when a chord is notated above a rest. For example, at times, voicing a 5-note chord on a rest may interfere with the melody line. For instance, if the top note of the 5-note chord is in the same area as the melody note that follows the rest. The sound of this high note in the 5-note chord could be heard as a deceptive or unclear melody note even though no melody note exists at the point of the rest. Therefore, a 4-note chord can be voiced with the top note of the chord well below the melody line that follows the rest and thus avoid any uncertainty in the melody line itself.

3. *By choice,* for example, because of the rich quality of sound produced in the middle register of the piano, the player has an option of playing a 4-note voicing that sounds rather than a 5-note voicing that sounds. For instance, (1) when harmonizing a melody note in the middle register; or (2) when voicing a chord, in the middle register, when a rest is given.

4. Also, the 4-note voicing can be applied to all chords; namely the Major, Minor, Minor 7th, Dominant 7th, and Diminished 7th chords. However, the player must remember that the 4-note chord is an optional voicing within the harmonic foundation of voicing 5-note chords.

E. Utilizing The Optional Four-Note Chord

The following Figure 65A illustrates the basic chords notated above melody notes to be harmonized. At this point, the player must realize that when a basic chord is notated above a melody note, the player is to embellish the chord according to the rules that pertain to that particular chord.

In addition, the melody line is specifically written in the low-middle register of the piano for the purpose of utilizing the optional 4-note chord as explained in letter "D". See Figure 65B, examples 1 and 2 for an illustration of harmonizing a melody embellishing the basic notated chords given in Figure 65A, and the utilization of the optional 4-note chord. Also, note the analysis precedes the figure.

Figure 65A

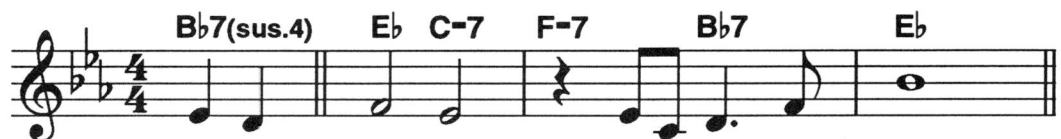

Analysis of a Harmonized Melody

Analysis of Figure 65B, examples 1 and 2:

1. Realize that when harmonizing a melody, the melody is harmonized on the exact beat on which the notated chord occurs by applying Steps 1 and 3 of the "method" in conjunction with #2 in letter "E" of each of the four types of chords discussed so far.

2. Realize that the basic notated chords, as given in Figure 65A, have been embellished throughout Figure 65B. Also note that the C-7 and the F-7 chords in example 1 are constructed within the rules of a 4-note voicing and are modern-sounding chords; therefore, they need not be embellished.

3. Realize that in example 1, in the pick up measure, the Bb9 (sus.4) that occurs on the 3rd beat is an optional 4-note chord. Also realize in example 2, in the pick up measure, the Bb9 (sus.4) that occurs on the 3rd beat, contains a 5-note chord; however, both chords sound. Therefore, as explained in #3, letter "D", the 4-note chord under these circumstances is a matter of choice.

4. Realize that in example 1, measure 1, the C-7 that occurs on the 3rd beat is an optional 4-note chord. Also realize that in example 2, measure 1, the C-7 that occurs on the 3rd beat contains a 5-note chord. However, the 5-note chord may be a little heavy and somewhat distorted in comparison to the 4-note chord. Therefore, as explained in #1, letter "D", the 4-note chord is one of necessity.

5.　Realize that in example 1, measure 2, the F-7 chord that occurs in the 1st beat at the rest is an optional 4-note chord. Also realize in example 2, measure 2, the F-9 that occurs on the first beat at the rest is a 5-note chord. However, the top note "G" in the 5-note chord is in the area of the melody. Therefore, as explained in #2, letter "D", the optional 4-note chord is one of necessity.

6.　Realize that in example 1, measure 2, the Bb7(b9) chord that occurs on the third beat is an optional 4-note chord. Also realize in example 2, measure 2, the Bb7(b9) that occurs on the third beat is a 5-note chord; however, the 5-note chord is too heavy. Therefore, as explained in #1, letter "D", the 4-note chord is of necessity.

7.　Realize the different types of chords used throughout the example, for instance, Major, Minor, Minor 7th and Dominant 7th.

8.　Realize that each chord voicing is a reflection of the material utilized in the "Amadiean Creed."

Figure 65B

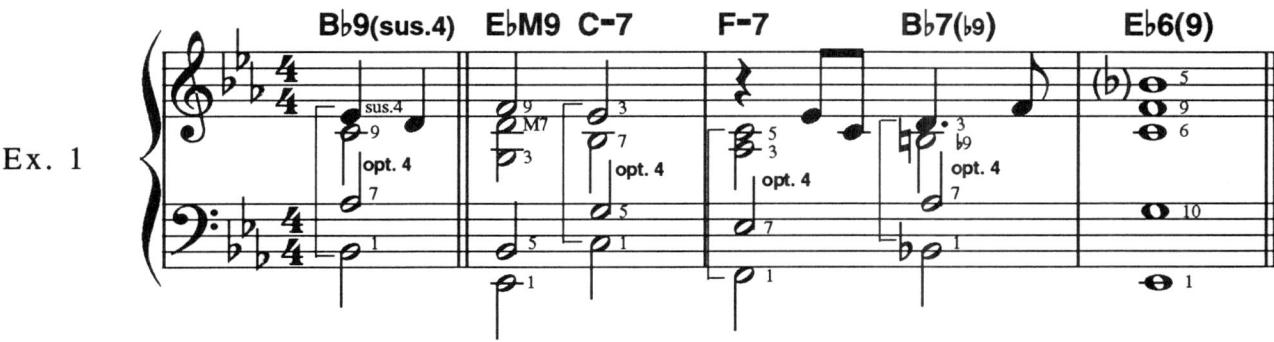

Ex. 1

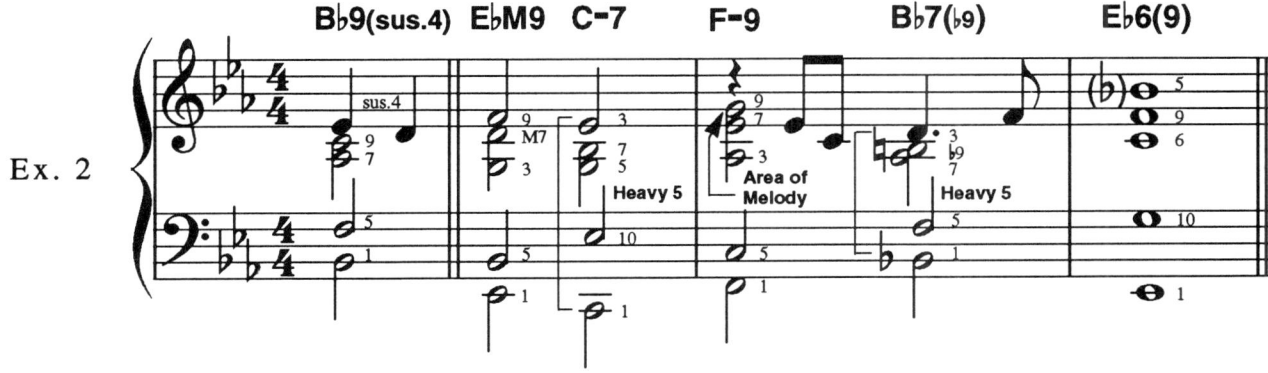

Ex. 2

F. Octave Displacement

Octave displacement, for our purpose, is the displacement of a melody note, up one octave, in order to avoid a heavy or distorted sounding chord when harmonizing the melody that is in the low-middle register of the piano. Although similar in purpose to the 4-note chord, the octave displacement is an additional tool that can be used when the 4-note chord is not effective.

The following Figure 66A illustrates two notes of a melodic line written in the low-middle register of the piano for the purpose of harmonizing the melody utilizing an octave displacement.

Figure 66A

Analysis of a Harmonized Melody

Analysis of Figure 66B, examples 1, 2 and 3:

1. Realize in example 1, the 5-note chords may be a little heavy and somewhat distorted.

2. Realize in example 2, the 4-note chords may be better; however, in example 3, the use of the octave displacement puts the melody in a better register and therefore the sound of the 5-note voicings is bright and full.

Figure 66B

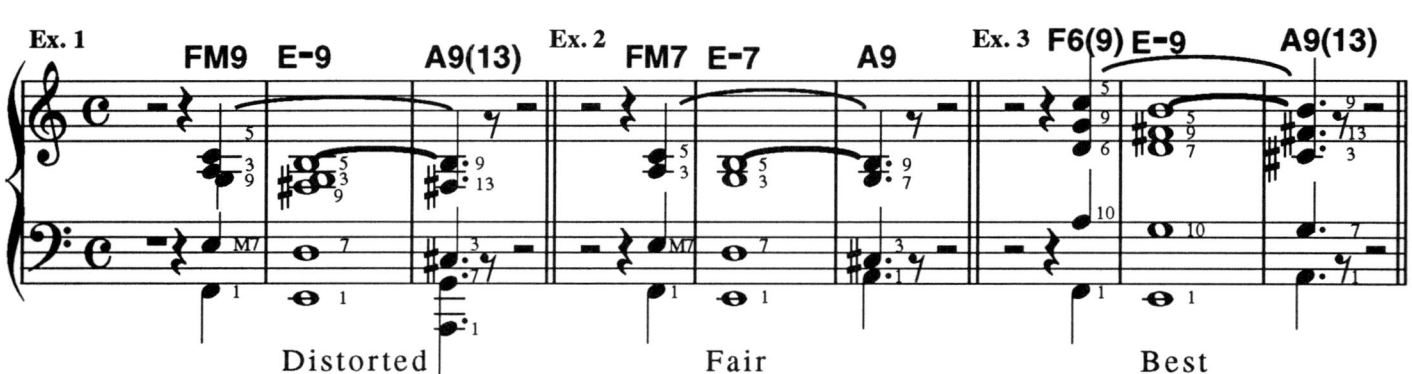

- 78 -

G. Utilizing the Octave Displacement and the Optional 4-Note Chord

The following Figure 67A illustrates basic chords notated above the excerpted melody of the composition "The Shadow Of Your Smile" to be harmonized. Notice the melody line occurs in the low-middle register of the piano and therefore gives us the opportunity to utilize the octave displacement explained in letter "F." See Figure 67B for an illustration utilizing the following: 1) an octave displacement and 2) the 4-note chord. Also, note the analysis precedes the figure.

Figure 67A

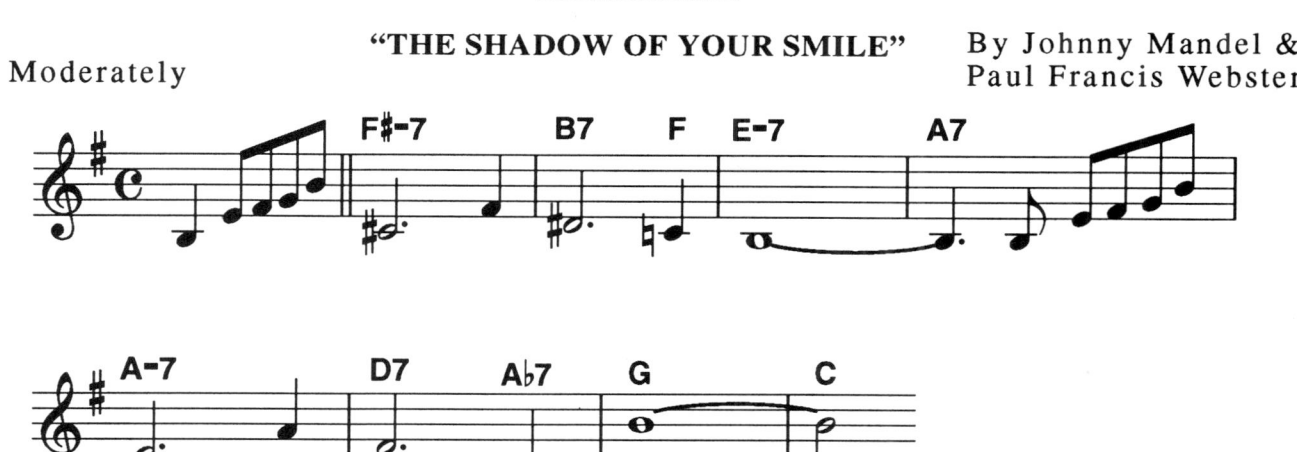

"THE SHADOW OF YOUR SMILE" By Johnny Mandel & Paul Francis Webster

Moderately

Analysis of a Harmonized Melody

Analysis of Figure 67B:

1. Realize that a 4-note voicings occurs in measure 1, on the F#-7 chord; also in measure 2, on the B7(♭9) chord.

2. Realize in measure 2, an octave displacement occurs as follows:

    a) on the 4th beat, on the note C, utilizing a 5-note voicing on the F6(9) chord.

    b) in measure 3, occurring on the 1st beat, on the note B, a 5-note voicing on the E-9 chord and also in measure 4, above the tied note B, occurring on the 1st beat using a 5-note voicing on the A9(13) chord.

3. Realize that when an octave displacement is used, it should continue to the end of the phrase. For example, in Figure 67B, the last note in the phrase occurs in measure 4, on the 1st beat, on the note B, the A9(13) chord.

4. Realize the melody notes and the chord voicings used in example 3 of Figure 66B occur in Figure 67B in measures 2, 3 and 4 (enclosed in bracket) for the purpose of illustrating the octave displacement in the context of a completed musical idea.

5. Realize that a 6-note voicing occurs on the 1st beat in measure 8, which is the result of voicing a 5-note chord underneath the tied melody note "B." Know that the 6-note chord voicing is an extension of the method and will be covered in Chapter VI.

6. Realize that each chord voicing is a reflection of the material utilized in the "Amadiean Creed."

Figure 67B

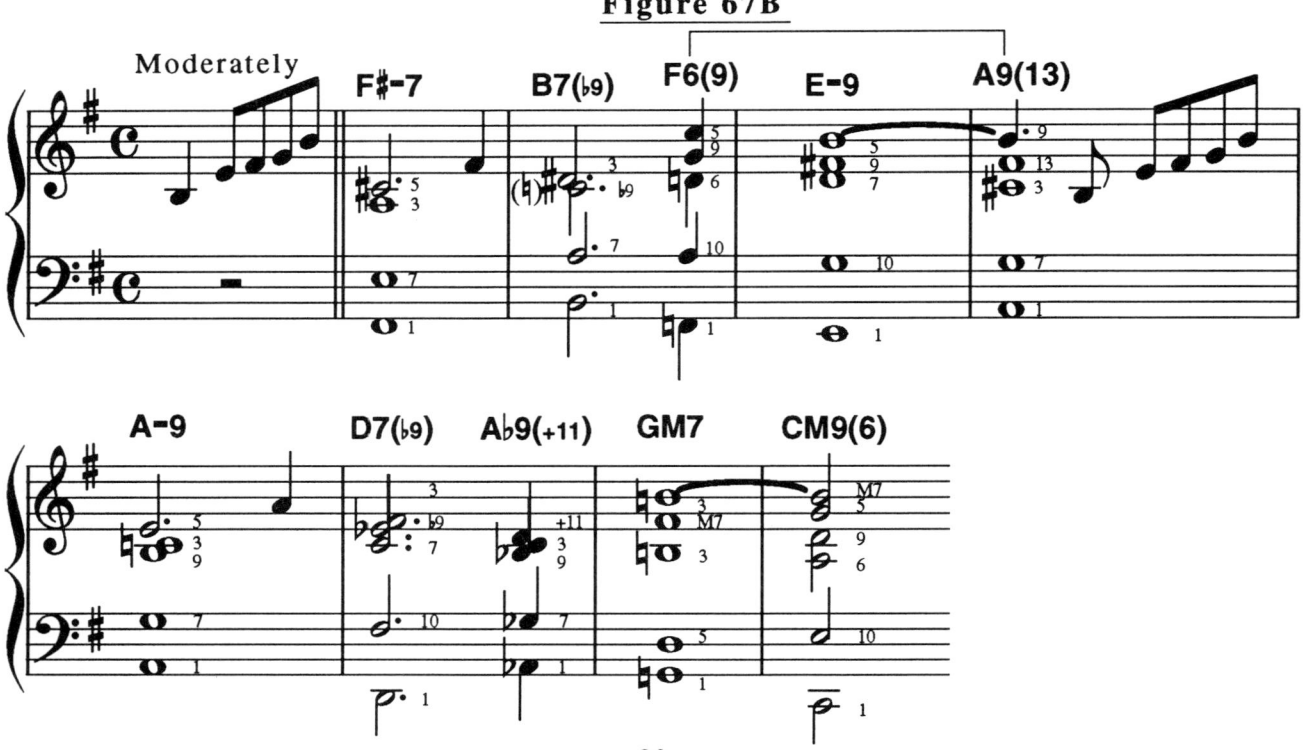

H. How to Deal With the Designated Bass Note in Notation

At times when a chord is notated, a composer or arranger will indicate in the notation a designated bass note other than the root to be the lowest note in the chord. For example see Figure 68A. The purpose of the designated bass note is to emphasize a particular sound and/or to preserve a bass line that is important to the music. See Figure 68B. Also, realize that the designated bass note can be indicated in all types of chords.

Procedure:

When a designated Bass note is indicated in the notation:

1. Put that designated note as the *lowest voice* of the chord.

2. Complete the bass voicing by choosing one note from the notes in the available bass voicings of that chord.

3. OR complete the bass voicing by doubling the melody note by putting that note in the bass voicing.

4. Under the melody note, add two notes to complete a 5-note chord voicing or add one note when choosing the optional 4-note chord voicing.

I. Illustration of the Designated Bass Note in Notation

The following Figure 68A illustrates the designated bass note indicated in notation. See Figure 68B for an illustration of harmonizing a melody utilizing the designated bass note in the notation. Also note the analysis precedes the figure.

Figure 68A

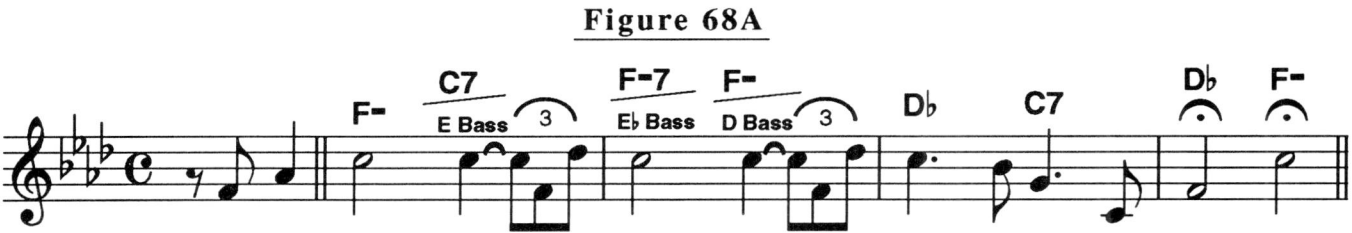

Analysis of a Harmonized Melody Utilizing the Designated Bass Note

Analysis of Figure 68B:

1. Realize that the designated bass note is the lowest note in the chord. See measures 1 and 2.

2. Realize the procedure (p.81) used to complete each bass voicing in measures 1 and 2 is as follows: in measure 1, the chord indicated C9 E bass, procedure #2 is applied. In measure 2, the chord indicated F-7 E♭ bass, procedure #3 is applied, and the chord indicated F-6(9) D bass, procedure #2 is applied.

3. Realize that under the melody note, two tones were added to complete the 5-note chord voicing.

4. Realize that the designated bass note appears in the Minor, Minor 7th and Dominant 7th chords.

5. Realize that each chord voicing is a reflection of the material utilized in the "Amadiean Creed."

Figure 68B

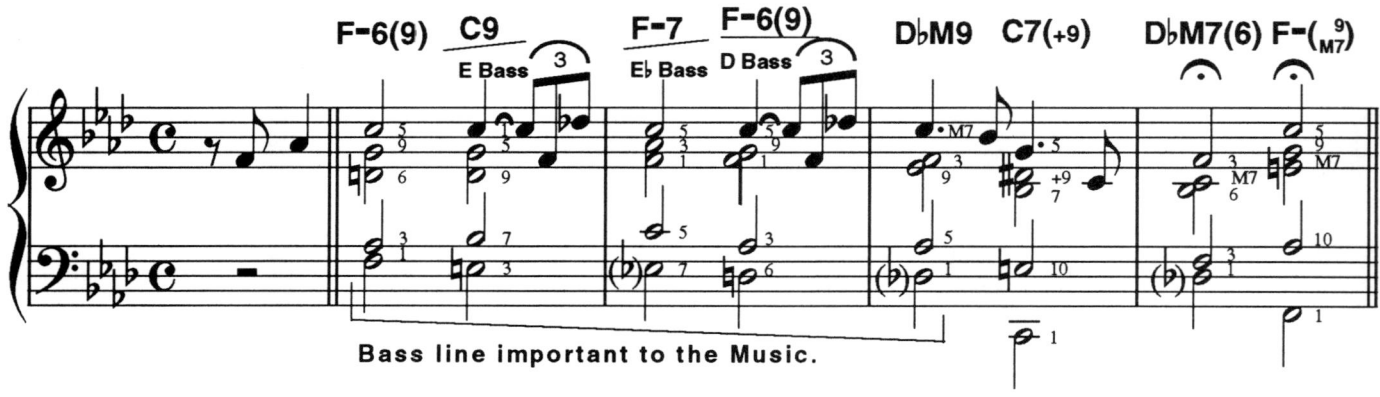

Bass line important to the Music.

J. Assignment: Harmonizing Melodies Using Major, Minor, Minor 7th, and Dominant Chords

Exercises 1 through 5

The following five exercises contain melody lines excerpted from original compositions except for example 2, which is the complete melody of "Tune Up" by Miles Davis. At this point, as the player applies the method throughout each exercise, he will realize his development as well as the potential of the method. Upon completion of the exercises, refer to *Appendix II Harmonized Melodies, Chapter IV, Exercises I through V*.

Harmonize the melodies in the following exercises embellishing the basic notated chords. The embellished chords must be notated above the basic chord where indicated in notation. Also indicate the content of each chord numerically.

"ALONE WITH YOU"

Slowly with a beat ♩ = 78

By Jimmy Amadie

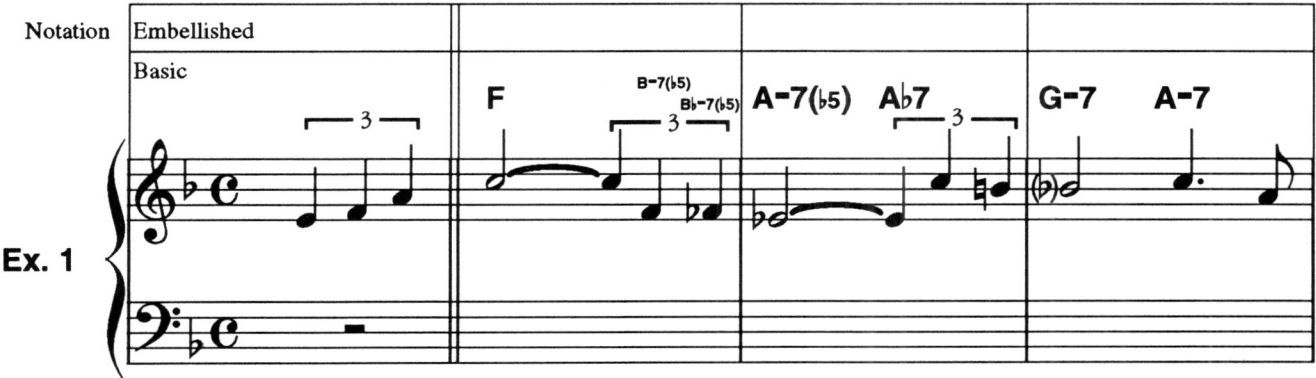

"TUNE UP"

Medium Up

By Miles Davis

Ex. 2

"SERENITY"

Slowly & leisurely ♩ = 63   By Jimmy Amadie

"DARK SHADOW"

Slowly ♩ = 60   By Jimmy Amadie

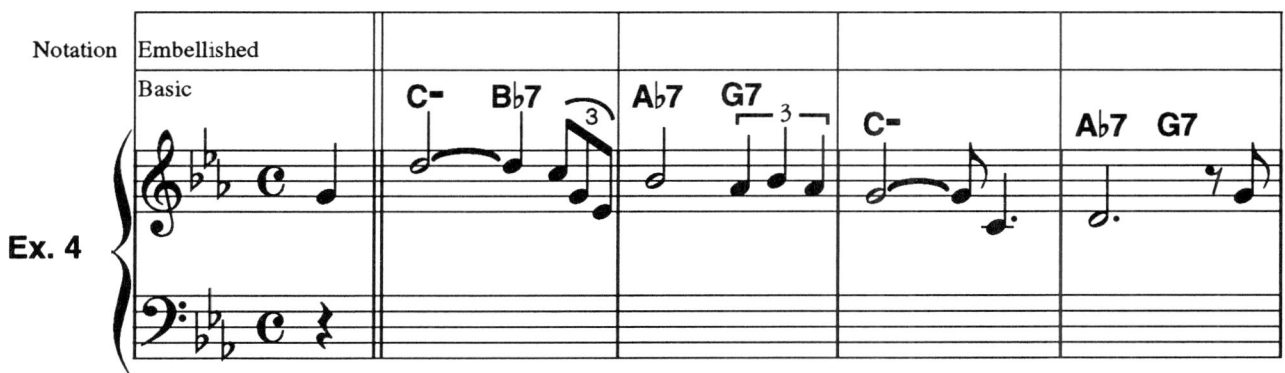

"SERENITY" ©1970,   "DARK SHADOW" ©1966,

"SWINGIN' EASY"

Medium Swing   By Jimmy Amadie

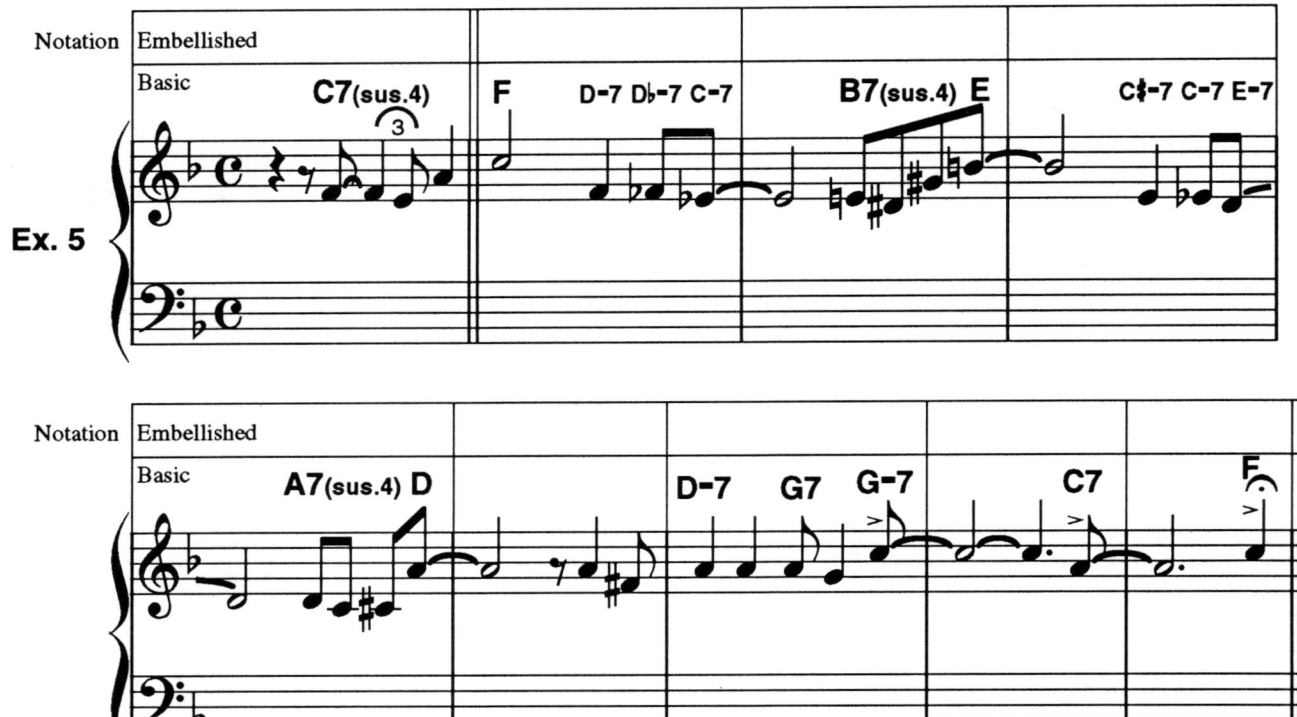

Summary: Now that the player has had ample opportunity to utilize the concept of the method by harmonizing the excerpted melodies of original compositions using Major, Minor, Minor 7th and Dominant 7th chords, it should be obvious that the Amadiean Creed clearly gives direction and purpose for which the method was created. With this in mind, our next chord, the Diminished 7th Chord, when utilized with the previous types of chords, will only serve to reinforce the method as the complete melodies of two original compositions are harmonized. Let us continue to progress by moving on to the final chord: the Diminished 7th Chord.

CHAPTER V - DIMINISHED CHORDS

PART I: PREPARATION FOR VOICING DIMINISHED CHORDS

A. Construction of Diminished Chords

A Diminished chord may be constructed by superimposing two intervals, a minor 3rd, and a diminished 5th above any note. The particular note chosen is termed the "root" of the chord.

Figure 69

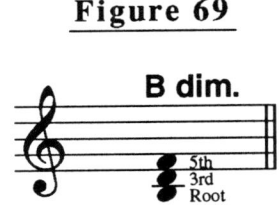

Also, a Diminished chord can be constructed on the 7th degree of a major scale by combining that degree termed "root" (1) of the chord and the following degrees located above that "root"; a 3rd and 5th.

Figure 70

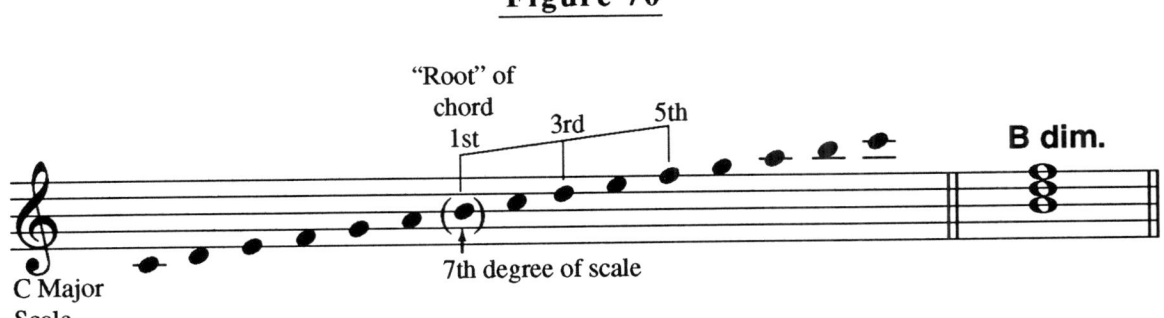

B. Embellishing a Diminished Chord

In popular music, standards, and jazz, when a Diminished chord is indicated, it may be embellished by adding the following note to the chord: the diminished 7th. Considering the root as the 1st degree of the chord, the added note is computed above that root. For example, the diminished 7th - seventh step above the root. In the opinion of the author, when a Diminished chord is indicated in notation, the diminished 7th note can automatically be added to the chord. Therefore it is possible to alter all Diminished chords to Diminished 7th chords.

Figure 71

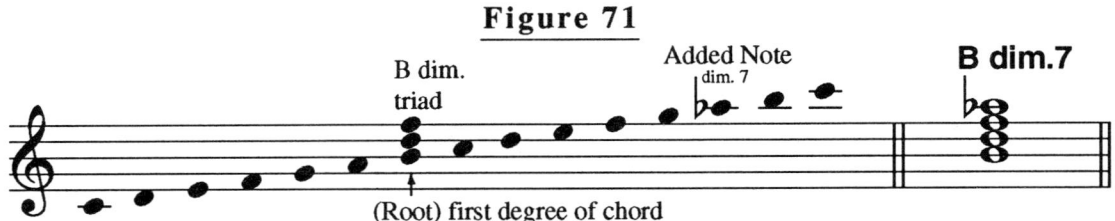

C. Notation of Diminished Chords

Diminished chords can be notated two ways: 1) "dim." and 2) the symbol (°) as in the following figure.

Figure 72

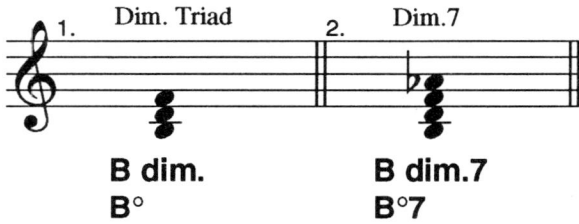

Content of the above Diminished 7th chords is as follows:

1. B dim. contains the root, minor 3rd above the root, and diminished 5th above the root.

2. B dim.7 contains the root, minor 3rd, diminished 5th and diminished 7th.

    Note: Hereafter, when numerically indicating the content of a diminished 7th chord, the diminished 5th and the diminished 7th are indicated °5 and °7 respectively. See Figure 73.

Also, note that a diminished 7th chord when inverted can produce a total of four different *root* name diminished 7th chords. In conclusion, realize that each of the inverted diminished 7th chords contain exactly the same notes; however, note that the root of the chord names the chord. See Figure 73.

Figure 73

The dim.7 chord inverted

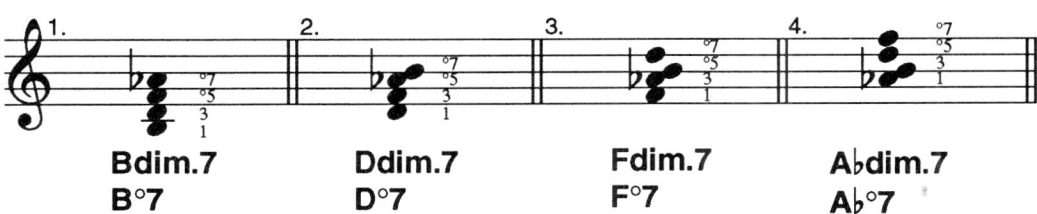

Bdim.7	**Ddim.7**	**Fdim.7**	**A♭dim.7**
B°7	**D°7**	**F°7**	**A♭°7**

D. Bass Voicings

A bass voicing consists of two notes. The bass voicings used when constructing a diminished 7th chord are as follows:

Figure 74

a. root and dim.5th

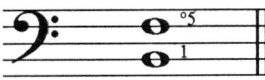

b. root and dim.7th

c. root and 10th

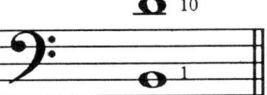

d. Optional - root and 3rd

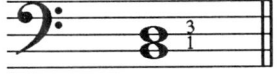

E. Rules for Voicing Diminished Chords

1. Alter all Diminished triads to Diminished 7th chords.

2. Use five (5) notes when voicing a Diminished 7th chord.

3. The root, 3rd, 5th and 7th must be present in the Diminished 7th chord.

4. Doubling is permitted as follows:

    Double one of the basic tones in the Diminished 7th chord to complete a 5-note chord voicing; however, do not exceed a total of five (5) notes in the chord voiced.

F. "Amadiean Creed": Method Used When Voicing Diminished 7th Chords

The method used to voice Diminished 7th chords is the "Amadiean Creed." Figure 75 and Figure 76 illustrate the construction of B dim.7th chord voicings by using the step-by-step application of the method. In addition, due to the Diminished 7th chord's limited content, the Diminished 7th chord is an easy and uncomplicated chord to learn; however, it also limits the player to only a handful of voicings. The result produces limited sounding chords as opposed to the varied voicings and rich quality of sound produced in the other types of chords learned. This is especially noticeable when learning the Diminished 7th chord in an isolated manner. Therefore, we suggest to the player that he reserve his opinion when learning the Diminished 7th chord until he develops his skill to utilize this chord in the context of a musical idea that encompasses the Diminished 7th and other types of chords. Also note in the following Figure 75 and Figure 76 each note is numerically indicated throughout each of the four steps so as to point out the exact relationship of each note in the chord.

Voicing a Diminished 7th chord using the Method (for example, B Diminished 7).

Figure 75

"AMADIEAN CREED"

Step 1 (2 notes)

Select a bass voicing as illustrated in letter D.
For example, the root and dim.5th.

Step 2 (add 1 note)

Put the 3rd in the chord if not present in the
bass voicing.

Step 3 (add 2 notes)

To complete the chord voicing, first put the remaining
available note into the dim.7th chord; the note is the
dim.7th. Second, double one of the basic notes in the
dim.7th chord as stated in the rules of letter E; here
they are the root, 3rd, dim.5th or the dim.7th. The note
chosen in Figure 75 is the dim.5th.

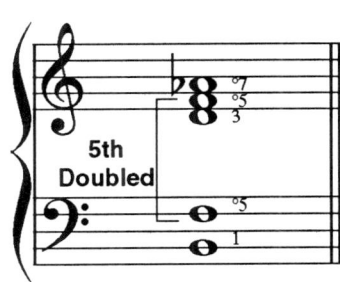

Step 4 (Notation)

Notate the chord above the staff. Realize the chord
results from applying the "Amadiean Creed": a 5-note
chord voicing. However, note that doubling is permitted
in the dim.7th chord. Play the chord.

Figure 76 illustrates the voicing of a B Diminished 7th chord using the "Amadiean Creed." However, note **Step 1**, when the 3rd has been selected in the bass voicing, or *indicated as the 10th*, for example, root and 3rd or root and 10th, the player needs to "adjust" **Step 2**. Furthermore, the adjustment of **Step 2**, as illustrated below, only occurs when the 3rd is selected in **Step 1**. Otherwise, **Step 2** of the "Amadiean Creed", as outlined in Figure 75, is *never* adjusted.

Figure 76

"AMADIEAN CREED"

Step 1 (2 notes)

Select a bass voicing as illustrated in letter D. For example, the root and 10th.

Step 2 (add 1 note)

Put the 3rd in the chord. However, when the 3rd is present in the bass voicing, "adjust" **Step 2** as follows: choose one note from the available notes which are derived from the rules in letter E; here they are the dim.5th and the dim.7th. Put the note chosen in one of the upper voices. For example, the note chosen in Figure 76 is the dim.7th.

Step 3 (add 2 notes)

To complete the chord voicing, first put the remaining available note in the dim.7th chord. The note is the dim.5th. Second, double one of the basic notes in the dim.7th chord. The note chosen in Figure 76 is the 3rd.

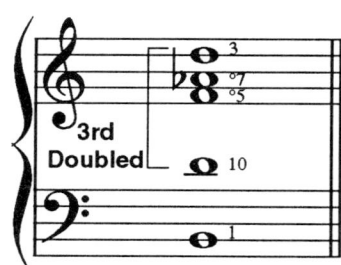

Step 4 (Notation)

Notate the chord above the staff. Realize the chord results from applying the "Amadiean Creed": a 5-note chord voicing. However, note that doubling is permitted in the dim.7th chord. Play the chord.

G. Examples of Diminished 7th Chord Voicings

Figure 77

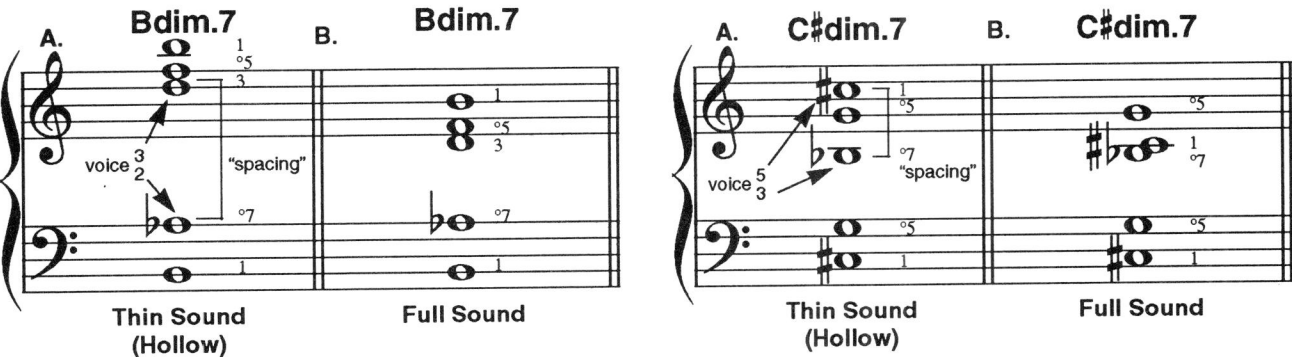

H. Rules Derived From Analysis: Spacing

"Spacing" (as mentioned in the previous chapters) is the result of having too much distance between one voice and another within the chord, thus causing the chord to sound thin or hollow. To avoid spacing in the Diminished 7th chord, do not exceed an interval of a 7th between the 2nd and 3rd voice in the chord or between the 3rd and 5th voice in the chord. For example, Figure 78A illustrates spacing between the second voice "Ab" and the third voice "D". The overall distance between the two voices is an augmented 11th, the result of which produces a hollow sounding chord. However, in Figure 78B, spacing is avoided as a result of not exceeding an interval of a 7th between the second and third voice. Realize that by moving the top three voices down an octave, the content of the chord remains the same, but the sound of the chord is improved. Figure 79A illustrates spacing between the third voice "Bb" and the fifth voice "C#". The overall distance between these two voices is an augmented 9th, the result of which produces a hollow sounding chord. However, in Figure 79B, spacing in avoided by not exceeding an interval of a 7th between the third and fifth voice within the chord. Realize that by changing the position of the third voice and the fifth voice in the chord, spacing is avoided and the sound of the chord is improved.

Figure 78   Figure 79

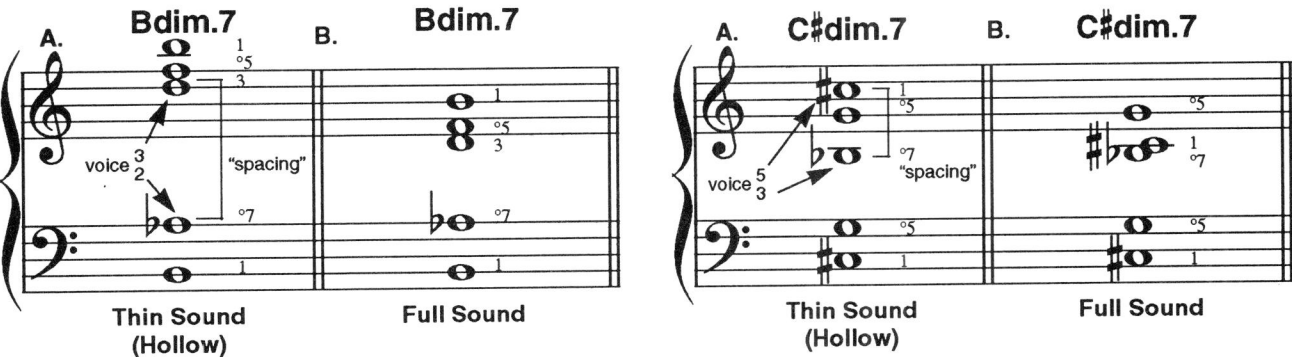

Now that the player has been given the background needed to construct Diminished 7th chord voicings, the player is ready to apply the method. To clearly emphasize the principle of the method, the following exercise is limited to the B dim.7th chords. However, the exercises that follow will cover all 12 Diminished 7th chords.

I.   ASSIGNMENT: CONSTRUCTING VOICINGS ON THE B DIMINISHED 7TH CHORD

Using Measure 1 as a guide, construct Diminished 7th chord voicings by applying the "Amadiean Creed." Realize that the Diminished 7th chord contains only four basic notes; therefore, it is difficult to achieve a variety of harmony. However, the player should vary the voicings as much as possible within the method. Also indicate the content of each chord numerically. Upon completion of the exercise, refer to *Appendix I Chord Voicings, Chapter V, Exercise I*. (Notice that from this point on, the text will be using the symbol (°) to denote "diminished" chords.)

<u>EXERCISE I</u>

"AMADIEAN CREED"

Step 1 (2 notes)

Select a bass voicing as illustrated in letter D.

Step 2 (add 1 note)

Put the 3rd in the chord if not present in the bass voicing. However, if the 3rd is chosen in the bass voicing, see **Figure 76** (Step 2).

Step 3 (add 2 notes)

To complete the chord voicing, first put the remaining available note into the dim.7th chord. Second, double one note as stated in letter E, p. 90. When completed, check for "spacing."

Step 4 (Notation)

Notate the chord above the staff. Realize the chord results from applying the "Amadiean Creed": a 5-note chord voicing. However, note that doubling is permitted in the dim.7th chord. Play the chord.

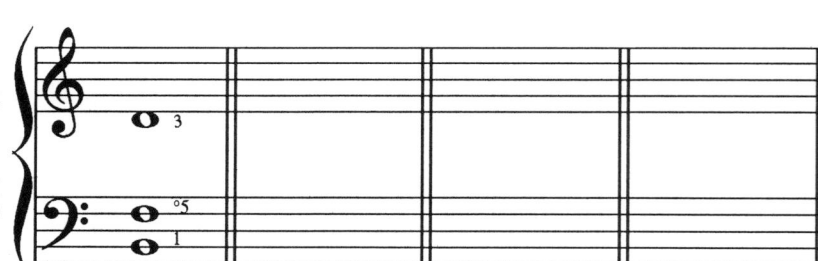

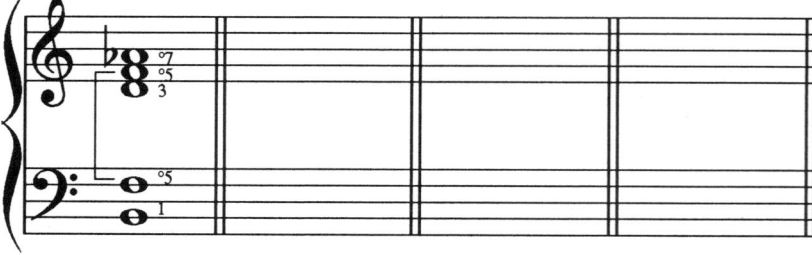

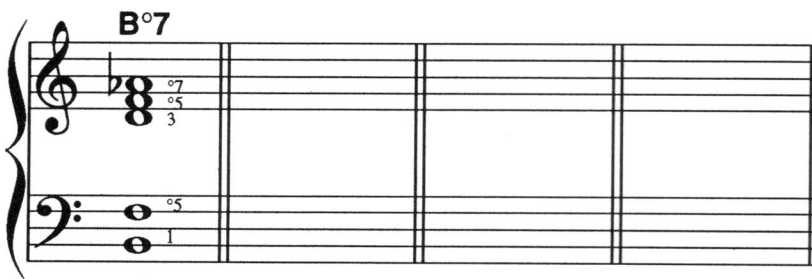

ASSIGNMENT: CONSTRUCTING VOICINGS ON THE REMAINING DIMINISHED 7TH CHORDS

   Using the voicings of your choice, construct the following Diminished 7th chords as indicated in the notation. Also indicate the content of each chord as illustrated in **measure 1**. See interpretation when reading "specific chord notation" Page 96, Letter A. Upon completion of the exercise, refer to *Appendix I Chord Voicings, Chapter V, Exercise II.*

EXERCISE II

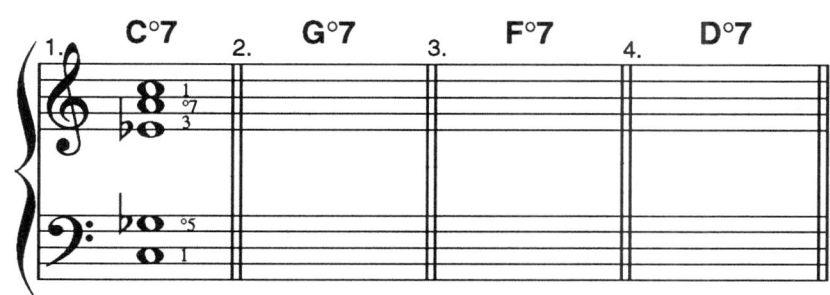

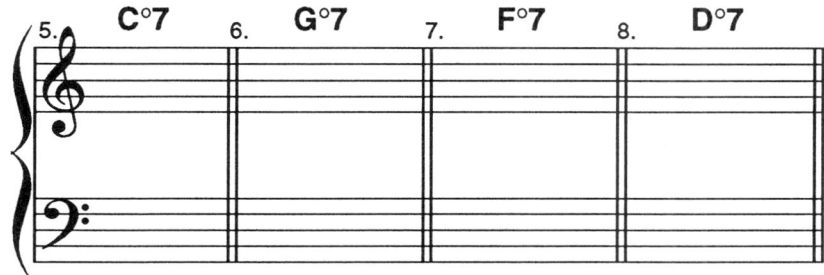

   Refer to *Appendix I* as stated above before beginning the additional writing exercises. For additional writing exercises: Construct 6 to 10 voicings of your choice on each of the following Diminished 7th chords:

C°7, G°7, F°7, D°7, B♭°7, A°7, E♭°7, E°7, A♭°7, B°7, D♭°7, F♯°7, C♭°7, C♯°7.

It is suggested that each assignment should consist of approximately four Diminished 7th chords.

PART II: INTERPRETATION AND PROCEDURE WHEN READING DIMINISHED CHORD NOTATION

A. Specific Chord Notation

When reading a specific chord notation of a Diminished 7th chord, for example, as in EXERCISE II, Page 95, the player should use only the content of the specific chord as indicated.

B. Basic Chord Notation

When reading basic chord notation of a Diminished chord, for example, as in EXERCISE III, Page 97, in the opinion of the author, the player should alter all basic Diminished chords to Diminished 7th chords.

C. Procedure for Sightreading Chord Notation in Tempo - Applying the "Amadiean Creed"

1. When sightreading chord notation, establish a slow tempo by counting a one measure rest.

2. As you count the measure rest in tempo, think of Steps 1, 2 and 3 of the "Amadiean Creed." Continuing in tempo, play the voicings of your choice holding each chord for 4 beats throughout the exercise.

3. When a mistake is made, Stop! Setting the tempo a little slower, count a one measure rest, allotting time to think of a voicing. Then voice the chord correctly in tempo.

D. Assignment: Sightreading Chord Notation

In Exercise III sightread the following Diminished triads, using the added note *in each chord*, for example, *the diminished 7th note*, to embellish the basic notated diminished triads. Follow the procedure for sightreading as indicated on *Page 96, Letter C.*

EXERCISE III

Play slowly

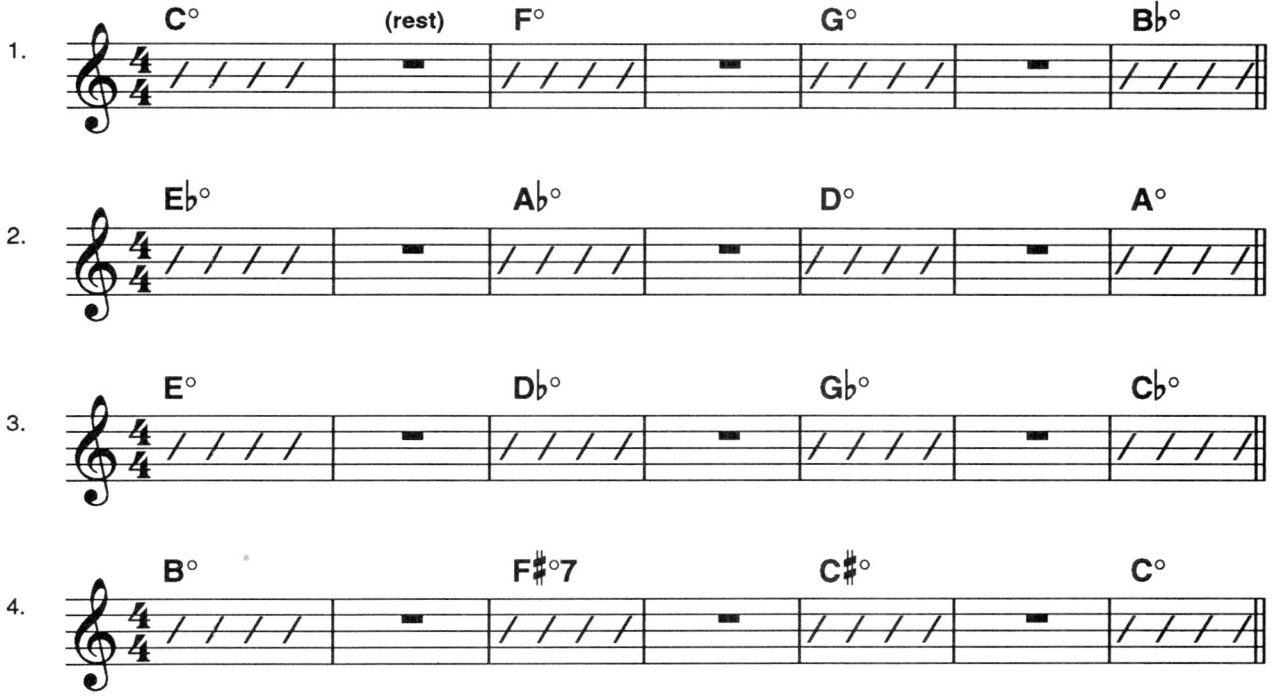

For additional sightreading exercises, read EXERCISE III in the following manner:

       1. RIGHT to LEFT (◄——) each line;

       2. From TOP to BOTTOM (↓) each column; and

       3. From BOTTOM to TOP (↑) each column.

If a player feels insecure about any particular Diminished 7th chords, he may, of course, formulate different series of Diminished 7th chords to overcome his weakness by stressing the more difficult ones.

PART III: INTRODUCTION TO HARMONIZATION OF A MELODY USING MAJOR, MINOR, MINOR 7TH, DOMINANT 7TH AND DIMINISHED 7TH CHORDS

Now that we have applied the method of constructing 5-note chord voicings to Diminished 7th chords, we are ready to harmonize a melody using the Diminished 7th chord. Also, in the examples that follow, melodies are harmonized utilizing the various types of chords learned thus far; namely, the Major, Minor, Minor 7th, Dominant 7th and Diminished 7th chords.

A. Background for Harmonization of a Melody: The "Harmonic Change"

In the following examples we will continue to apply the principle of the harmonic change (indicated in bracket) as stated in the previous chapters. For example, Figure 80A, measure 1: the FM9 occurs on the first beat above the note "C" - also the following notes "C" and "A" (enclosed in bracket) pertain to the FM9 harmony. Also in measure 1 the A-7 occurs on the third beat above the note "G". Finally, the Ab°7 occurs on the fourth beat above the note "F". In measure 2, the G-7 occurs on the first beat above the note "Bb" and the following note "D" (enclosed in bracket) pertains to the G-7 harmony. Also in measure 2, the A-9 occurs on the third beat above the note "E", the Ab°7 above the note "F", the C7 (b9) above the note "G". In measure 3, the GbM7(6) occurs on the first beat above the note "F". Also in measure 3, the FM9(6) occurs on the third beat above the note "G". Realize that the bracket encloses all beats that pertain to the same harmony. See Figure 80B for an illustration of harmonizing the melody given in Figure 80A. Also note the analysis precedes the figure.

Figure 80A

B. Analysis of the Procedure Used to Harmonize a Melody

Analysis of Figure 80B:

1. Each chord voicing occurs on the exact beat on which the chord is notated (harmonic change) indicated by (⬇———┐) left side of bracket.

2. The melody note appears in the top voice of the chord; also, the melody notes that follow remains within the framework of that same harmony (enclosed in bracket) until the new harmonic change occurs.

3. Under the given melody note, at the point where the chord is notated, a bass voicing consisting of two notes is inserted in the bass, indicated by (┛).

4. Two more tones indicated by (◄———) are added to complete the 5-note chord voicing.

5. Realize that each chord voicing is a reflection of the material utilized in the "Amadiean Creed."

Figure 80B

- 99 -

C. Special Rules for Doubling

As previously stated when constructing a diminished 7th chord, doubling one note is necessary to complete a 5-note chord voicing. Also, when the root, 3rd, 5th or the 7th of the diminished 7th chord is the melody note, the melody note can be doubled. See Figure 81, Ex. 1 and Ex. 2. Note: "Spacing" is permitted only when the melody is doubled in the 3rd and 5th voice. See Figure 81, Ex. 2.

Figure 81

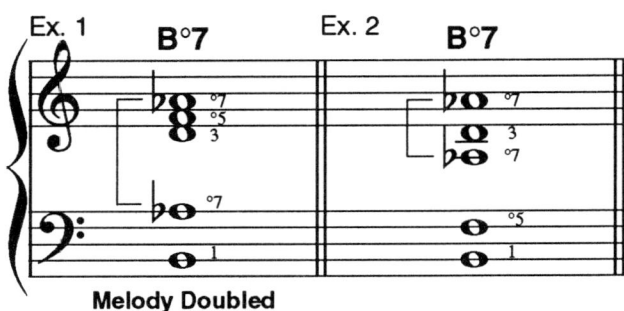

Melody Doubled

D. Utilizing Doubling of a Melody Note

The following Figure 82A illustrates basic chords notated above melody notes to be harmonized. See Figure 82B for an illustration of harmonizing the melody embellishing the basic notated chords given in Figure 82A. Also note the analysis precedes the figure.

Figure 82A

Analysis of a Harmonized Melody

Analysis of Figure 82B:

1. Realize that the melody is harmonized on the exact beat on which the notated chord occurs by applying Steps 1 and 3 of the "method" in conjunction with #2 in letter E, of each of the five types of chords discussed so far.

2. Realize that each of the basic notated chords as given in Figure 82A has been embellished throughout Figure 82B.

3. Realize that in measure 1, the BbM9 chord that occurs on the first beat above the rest is a 5-note chord. Also realize that in measure 3, the G-7 chord that occurs on the first beat above the rest is an optional 4-note chord.

4. Realize that in measure 2, the A-7 and Ab°7 chords illustrate melody notes being doubled in each chord.

5. Realize that each chord voicing is a reflection of the material utilized in the "Amadiean Creed."

Figure 82B

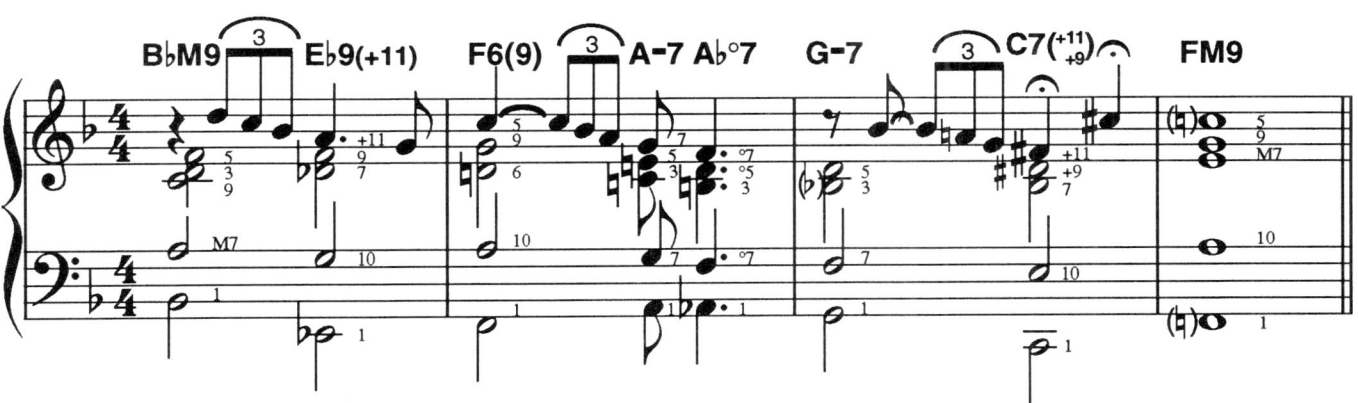

E. Melody Notes Non-Related to the Chord

A non-related melody note, as previously defined, is a melody note that is not part of the basic chord nor found to be an embellished note of that chord.

The following Figure 83A illustrates a melody line that contains non-related notes that are to be harmonized. See Figure 83B for an illustration harmonizing non-related notes. Also note the analysis precedes the figure.

Figure 83A

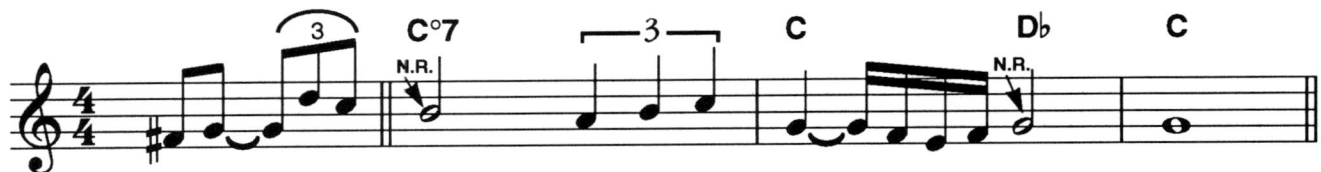

Analysis of a Harmonized Melody

1. Realize that Figure 83B is an illustration of harmonizing the melody given in Figure 83A.

2. Realize that the basic notated chords, as given in Figure 83A, have been embellished in Figure 83B.

3. Realize that non-related melody notes are harmonized in measures 1 and 2.

4. Realize the different types of chords used throughout the example, for instance, Major and Diminished 7th Chords.

5. Realize that each chord voicing is a reflection of the material utilized in the "Amadiean Creed."

Figure 83B

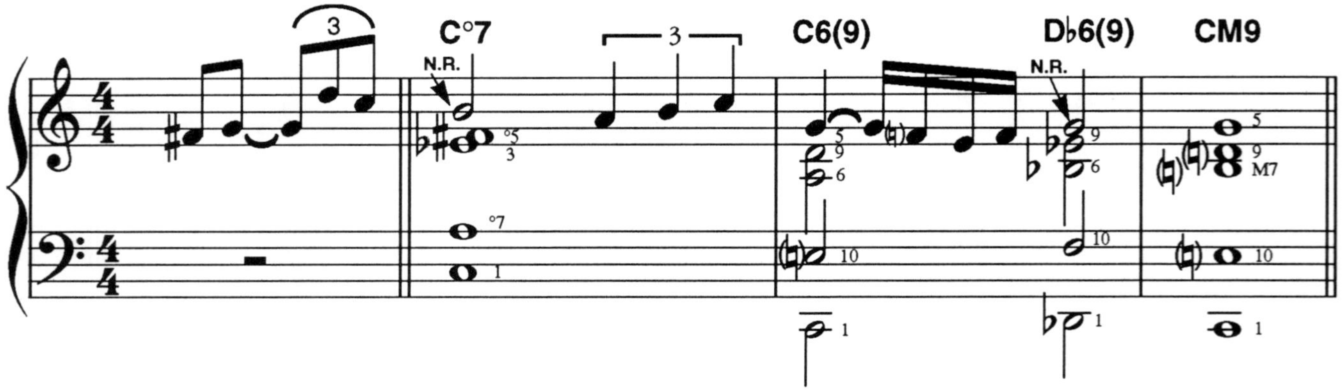

F. Assignment: Harmonizing the Melody of Two Compositions Using Major, Minor, Minor 7th, Dominant 7th and Diminished 7th Chords.

COMPOSITIONS 1 & 2

The following exercises contain the melody lines of two original compositions. This material offers the player the opportunity to utilize the harmonic concept of the method introduced in this text as it applies to each of the various chords. Upon completion of the exercises, refer to *Appendix II, Harmonized Melodies, Chapter V, Compositions 1 and 2.*

Harmonize the melodies in the following exercises embellishing the basic notated chords. The embellished chords must be notated above the basic chord where indicated in notation. Also indicate the content of each chord numerically.

COMPOSITION 1
"YOU'RE THE ONE FOR ME"

Slowly with a beat ♩ = 78   By Jimmy Amadie

COMPOSITION II
"DARK SHADOW"

Slowly ♩ = 60

By Jimmy Amadie

CHAPTER VI - EXPANDING THE METHOD UTILIZING PRACTICAL CONCEPTS

The purpose of Chapter VI is to illustrate that the "method" of using 5-note chord voicings can serve as the harmonic foundation upon which 6-note and 7-note chord voicings can be acquired, therefore expanding the concept of the "Amadiean Creed." For examples illustrating the expansion of the "method" see Figure 85, following the analysis in letter "C".

A. Six-Note Chord Voicings

A six-note chord can be an additional tool and an extension of the method; however, the player needs to use his own judgment and taste in determining whether or not the situation warrants 6-note chords. Voicing a 6-note chord can be used as follows:

1. To enrich harmony thereby thickening the voicing with an additional tone without doubling.

2. To reinforce the melody by doubling only the melody note in the chord.

3. To reinforce a minor 7th chord by doubling either the 5th or the 7th of the chord.

B. Seven-Note Chord Voicings

The seven-note chord is also an extension of the method. Although used less frequently than the 6-note chord, it is very effective. Realize the difference between the 6-note chord and the 7-note chord is that the bass voicing in the 7-note chord consistently contains three notes in each chord. The following examples illustrate the *various bass voicings* that can be used in a 7-note chord for each of the various types of chords. Notice the similarity that exists throughout each of the examples.

Figure 84

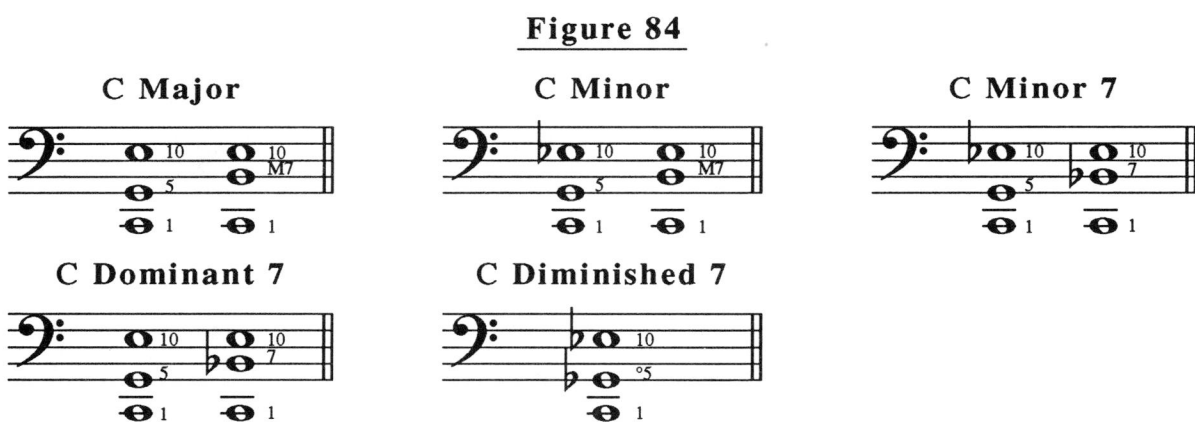

C Major   C Minor   C Minor 7

C Dominant 7   C Diminished 7

C. Utilizing Five-Note, Six-Note and Seven-Note Chord Voicings

The following Figure 85A illustrates basic chords notated above the excerpted melody of the composition "You're The One For Me" to be harmonized. See Figure 85B for an illustration of harmonizing the melody utilizing the following: 1) the "method" of 5-note chord voicings, 2) expanding the method to 6-note chord voicings, 3) expanding the method to 7-note chord voicings.

Figure 85A

"YOU'RE THE ONE FOR ME"   By Jimmy Amadie

Slowly

Analysis of a Harmonized Melody

Analysis of Figure 85B, Examples 1, 2 and 3:

1. Realize that the basic notated chords, as given in Figure 85A, have been embellished within the rules of the "method" in examples 1, 2 and 3 of Figure 85B.

2. Realize in example 1, 5-note voicings are used; in example 2, 6-note voicings and in example 3, 7-note voicings.

3. Realize that only the chords in example 1 are numerically indicated throughout the figure. The reason for this is that each chord in examples 2 and 3 contains the same basic 5 notes indicated in example 1. However, as the method is expanded to 6 notes, as in example 2, and 7 notes, as in example 3, realize that only those additional tones are numerically indicated for the purpose of pointing out to the player the manner in which the method was expanded.

4. Realize that 6-note and 7-note chords afford the player the flexibility to open up the sound of the harmony when needed.

Figure 85B

Slowly

Ex. 1

Ex. 2

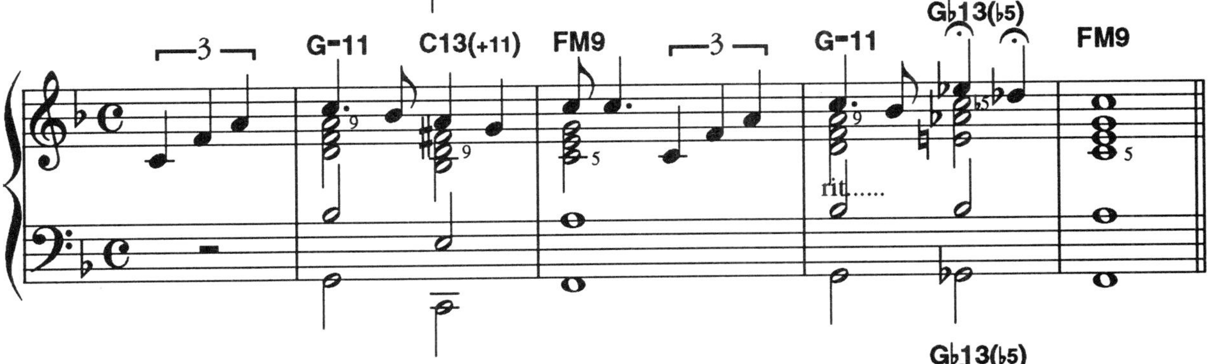

Ex. 3

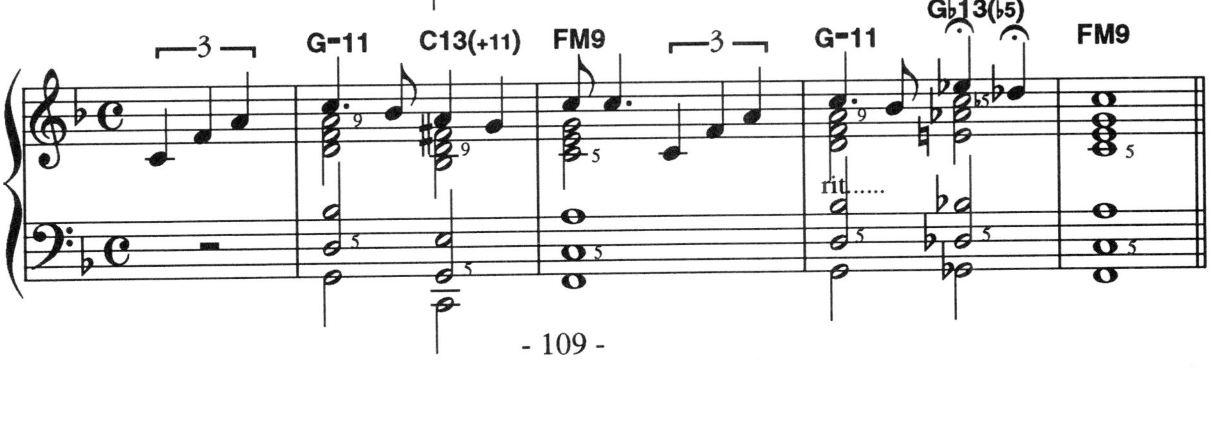

D. Harmonizing the Major 7th and the Root as Melody Notes in Major and Minor Chords through Specific Chord Voicings

In the following Figure 86, Example 1 illustrates specific voicings when the Major 7th is the melody note is a Major chord. Example 2 illustrates when the Major 7th is the melody note is a Minor chord. The following Figure 87, Example 1 illustrates specific voicings when the root is the melody note in a Major chord; Example 2, when the root is the melody note in a Minor chord. Also realize other voicings are possible and therefore the player is free to experiment on his own.

Figure 86   **Figure 87**

Major 7th as the melody note   Root as the melody note

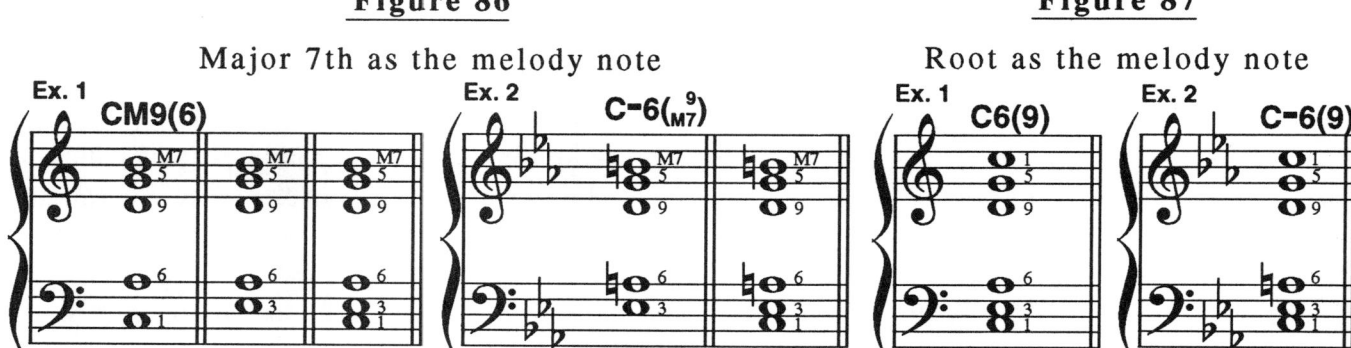

E. Utilizing Specific Chord Voicings and Six-Note Chord Voicings

The following Figure 88A illustrates basic chords notated above the excerpted melody of the composition "I Can't Get Started" to be harmonized. Also realize that measure 3 is an additional measure and was inserted for the purpose of utilizing a "specific chord voicing." See Figure 88B for an illustration of harmonizing the melody utilizing the following: 1) specific chord voicings, 2) Six-note chord voicings. Also, note the analysis precedes the figure.

Figure 88A

Slowly   "I CAN'T GET STARTED"   By Gershwin & Duke

Analysis of a Harmonized Melody

Analysis of Figure 88B:

1. Realize that the basic notated chords, as given in Figure 88A, have been embellished within the rules of the "method" in Figure 88B.

2. Realize the use of the "specific chord voicing" when the Major 7th is the melody note in the major chord. See measures 1 and 3.

3. Realize the use of the "specific chord voicing" when the root is the melody note in the major chord. See measure 4.

4. Realize that the method has been expanded to 6-note chords throughout; however, notice the 5-note chord, the D-9. Even though a 6-note chord is possible, the 5-note chord may be more effective. Therefore, judgment and personal taste must be the determining factors for expanding the "method".

Figure 88B

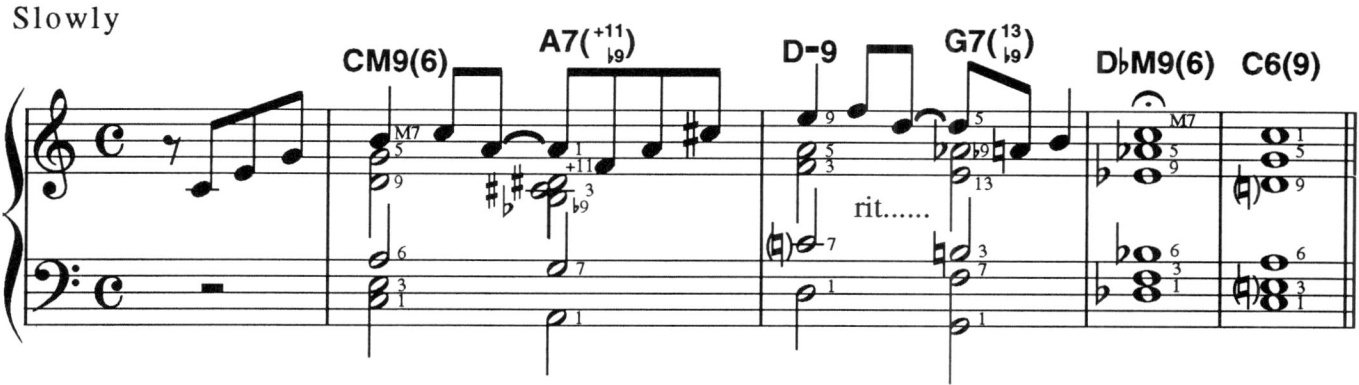

F. Special Circumstances Permitting the Augmented 11th in a Major Chord

Realize that it is possible to use an Augmented 11th in a Major Chord when the Major Chord is the final chord in the music and when its presence does not disturb the overall quality of the harmony in that final chord. Also, in this situation, the augmented 11th could be considered an embellished tone to the chord; however, realize that the augmented 11th is *not* part of the basic harmony of a major chord nor is it an embellished tone that can be used freely when major chords are notated other than as described above.

G. Utilizing Five-Note, Six-Note and Seven-Note Chord Voicings and the Augmented 11th in a Major Chord

The following Figure 89A illustrates basic chords notated above the excerpted melody of the composition "Laura" to be harmonized. Also realize that in measures 7 and 8 an additional melody was inserted to create an ending for the purpose of expanding the "method." See Figure 89B for an illustration of harmonizing the melody utilizing the following: 1) 5-note, 6-note and 7-note chord voicings 2) the augmented 11th in a Major chord. Also note the analysis precedes the figure.

Figure 89A

"LAURA"   By Johnny Mercer & David Raskin

Analysis of a Harmonized Melody

Analysis of Figure 89B:

1. Realize that the basic notated chords, as given in Figure 89A, have been embellished within the rules of the "method" in Figure 89B.

2. Realize that in measures 3 and 4 of Figure 89A, the G Major chord is notated; however, in measure 3 of Figure 89B the author took the liberty of inserting an A–9 chord (a "passing chord") between the G Major chords. The passing chord will be explained in Chapter VII.

3. Realize the melody has been changed in measure 7 and 8 for the purpose of using the Augmented 11th in the Major chord notated $FM9(^{13}_{+11})$. Also, the 6th is usually indicated as the 13th when the augmented 11th is present in a major chord.

4. Realize the 6-note voicings utilized in measure 2 the $D13(^{+11}_{b9})$, in measure 3 the GM9(6), and in measure 6 the $C13(^{+11}_{+9})$ and the 7-note voicings utilized in measure 7 the FM9(6), $F\#9(^{13}_{b5})$, and in measure 8 the $FM9(^{13}_{+11})$ are an extension of the method.

Figure 89B

Moderately

CHAPTER VII - SOME THEORETICAL CONSIDERATIONS

The purpose of this chapter is to deal with some of the basic theoretical concepts that have become common practice in modern harmony; therefore, know that it is not the intention of this writer, nor is it within the scope of this text, to cover *all* the concepts that do exist. However, the concepts introduced will be discussed and illustrated as we continue to develop and expand the use of the "method" - the purpose for which this book is intended. Also, at times Roman Numerals will be used to indicate the corresponding scale degrees upon which the chord is built.

A. Passing Chord

A passing chord is a chord that occurs between two chords of the given harmony of a composition, for the purpose of creating motion and/or to introduce a harmonic color that may or may not be related to the fundamental harmony of the composition.

For example, when a major chord, the tonic (I) is indicated for two measures, as in the G Major in example I, a common practice is to use a minor 7th chord, located on the second degree (II-7), above the root of the major chord, as a passing chord, for example the A-7, as illustrated in example 2. (For an earlier example, see Figure 89B, measure 3). Also, when a major chord, the tonic (I) is indicated for one measure, as in the G Major in example 3, and the following measure contains a minor 7th chord located on the third degree (III-7) above the tonic (I), for example the B-7, it is another common practice to use the II-7 chord as a passing chord as illustrated in example 4.

Figure 90

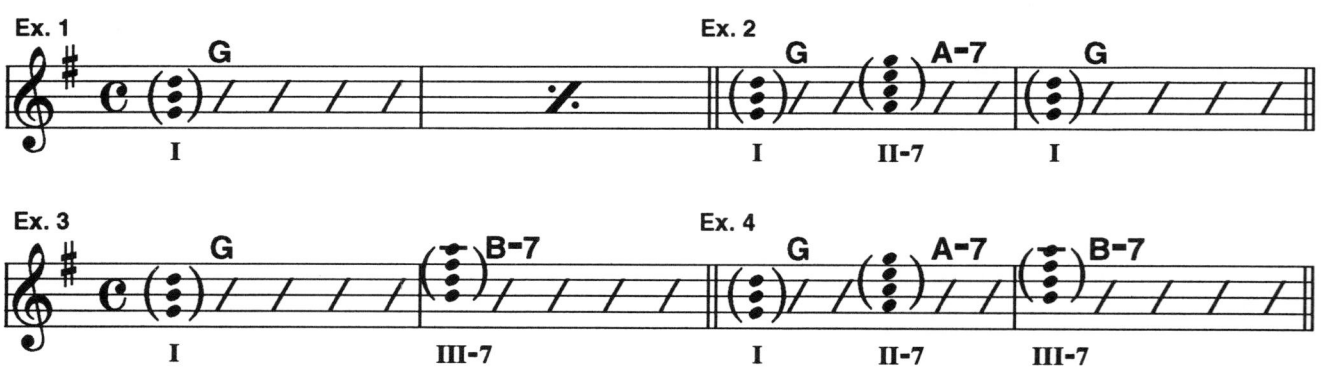

B. Substitute Chord

The substitute chord is an additional tool that affords the player the option of substituting a chord in place of another chord, thereby changing the chords of a composition rather than using those indicated in the sheet music and/or in the fakebook.[1] Some of the reasons for this are:

1. The notated chords indicated most often reflect the content of the arrangement, thereby limiting the player to those chords contained in sheet music.

2. To avoid using the same chords repeatedly.

[1] Fakebooks contain single line melodies of compositions with no bass accompaniment. In them the chords notated above the melody are usually derived from the chords in the standard sheet music.

3. To add variety within the concept of the basic harmony.

4. To expand the harmonic concept beyond the basic context of the harmony.

To illustrate the function of a substitute chord, we will deal with substitute chords for the dominant 7th chord. For our purpose, we will illustrate two of the substitute chords most often used for the dominant 7th chord such as:

The Minor 7th Chord and The Dominant 7th Chord on the Flatted Fifth

1. **The Minor 7th Chord**

Substitute the minor 7th chord located on the perfect 5th above the root of the dominant 7th chord when a dominant 7th chord is indicated. The following Figures 91 and 93 illustrate various ways in which the substitute minor 7th chord can be used. See the analyses preceding the figures.

Analysis of Figures 91, 92 and 93:

- Figure 91, Example 1, contains the dominant 7th chord, G7.

- Example 2 contains the substitute chord D-7 occurring on the first beat in place of the G7. Realize the D-7 chord (II-7) resolves to the G7 chord (V7) on the 3rd beat, to the chord for which it was substituted. Realize the number of beats that each chord receives is usually divided evenly between the two chords. Also, realize that the movement of a II-7 chord to a V7 chord produces a basic harmonic progression which is derived from the major scale, as illustrated in Figure 92.

- Figure 93, Example 1, contains a G7 chord for two measures.

- Examples 2, 3 and 4 illustrate the various ways in which the substitute chord, the minor 7th (II-7) and the dominant 7th chord (V7) can be broken down.

Figure 91   Figure 92

Figure 93

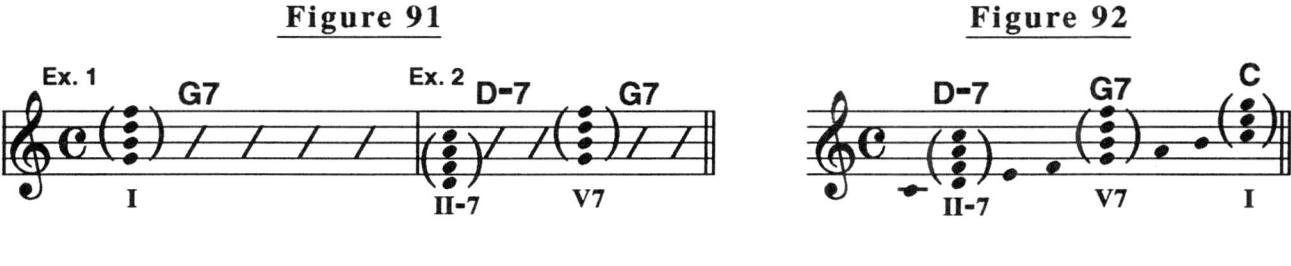

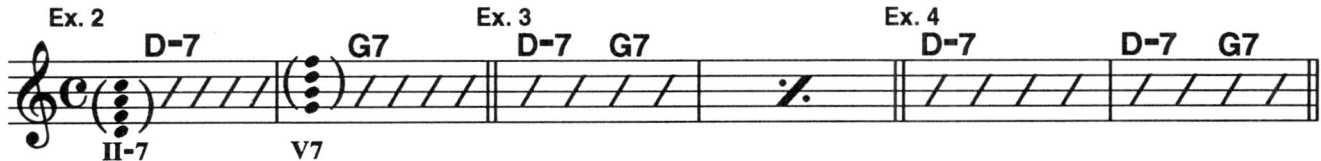

2. The Dominant 7th Chord on the Flatted Fifth

Substitute the dominant 7th chord, located on the flatted fifth above the root of the dominant chord, when a dominant 7th chord is indicated. The following Figure 94 illustrates various ways in which the substitute dominant 7th chord on the flatted fifth can be used. See the analysis preceding the figure.

Analysis of Figure 94:

- Figure 94, Example 1, contains the dominant 7th chord G7 (V7) resolving to C Major, the (I).

- Example 2 contains the substitute chord D♭7 (♭II7) occurring on the 3rd beat in place of the G7 chord. Realize the D♭7 chord resolves to the C Major chord.

- Example 3 contains the substitute chord D♭7 occurring on the 1st beat in place of the G7 chord.

- Example 4 contains two substitute chords. The A♭-7 (♭VI-7) chord is the substitute for D♭7 chord, and the D♭7 chord is the substitute for the G7 chord.

Figure 94

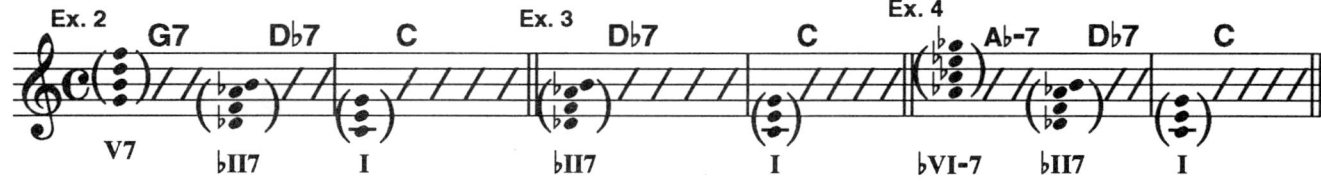

In conclusion, the two substitute chords may be contrasted as follows:

1. Realize the minor 7th chord, as a substitute chord, adds variety within the context of the basic harmony and therefore seldom causes conflict when used.

2. Realize the dominant 7th chord on the flatted fifth, as the substitute chord for the dominant 7th chord, changes the basic context and therefore, in comparison to the minor 7th chord, its use is limited.

3. Realize that the effective use of substitute chords depends on taste and good judgment, not on technical correctness.

C. Interpretation of the Minor 6th Chord When Preceding a Dominant 7th Chord

When a Minor 6th chord precedes a dominant 7th chord by a whole step, for example F-6 to G7, interpret the 6th of the minor 6th chord as the root of the chord; however, realize that the minor 6th chord is changed into a minor 7th chord with a flat 5. To illustrate this procedure, Figure 95, Example 1 contains an F-6 (IV-6) chord to G7 (V7); however, notice in Example 2, the 6th of the minor chord, when interpreted as the root of the chord, changes the construction of the chord to a D F A♭ C which thereby produces a D-7(♭5) (II-7(♭5)) chord. Therefore realize that when a minor 6th chord precedes a dominant 7th chord by a whole step, the minor 6th chord is *changed* into a minor 7th with a flat 5 as illustrated. Also, realize the interpretation of the Minor 6th chord as described above, produces a basic harmonic progression; for example, the movement of a II-7(♭5) chord to a V7 chord which is derived from the harmonic minor scale as illustrated in Figure 96.

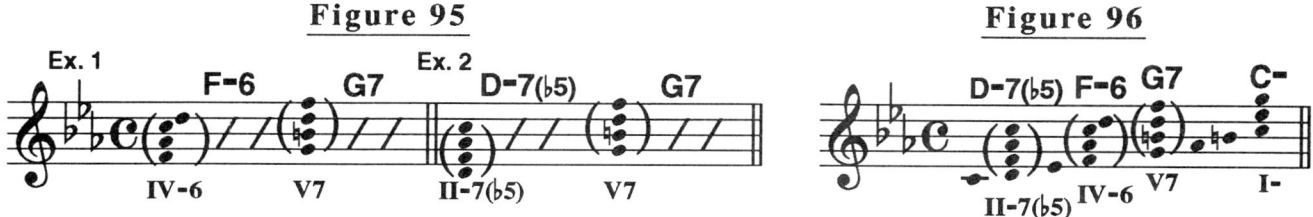

D. Utilizing Substitute Chords; Interpretation of the Minor 6th Chord When Preceding a Dominant 7th Chord; Five-Note, Six-Note and Seven-Note Chord Voicings

The following Figure 97A illustrates basic chords notated above the excerpted melody of the composition "Don't Blame Me", to be harmonized. Also, realize that in measures 8, 9 and 10 an additional melody was inserted to create an ending for our purpose of expanding the "method". See Figure 97B for an illustration of harmonizing the melody utilizing the following: 1) substitute chords, 2) the interpretation of the Minor 6th chord and 3) expanding the "method". Also note the analysis precedes the figure.

Figure 97A

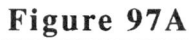

Moderately   "DON'T BLAME ME"   By Dorothy Fields & Jimmy McHugh

Analysis of a Harmonized Melody

Analysis of Figure 97B:

1. Realize that the basic notated chords, as given in Figure 97A, have been embellished within the rules of the "method" in Figure 97B.

2. Realize that substitute chords are used in measures 1 and 2. For example, the F-7 chord in measure 1 occurring on the 3rd beat is the substitute chord for the B♭7 chord indicated in measure 1 of Figure 97A. Also, the E-7 chord in measure 2 occurring on the 1st beat is the substitute chord for the A7 chord indicated in measure 2 of Figure 97A. Notice each substitute chord resolves to the dominant 7th chord for which it was substituted. For example, F-7(11) to B♭7(13) and E-11 to A7(⁺¹¹♭9).

3. Realize that in measures 3, 5 and 6, the Minor 6th chord preceding the dominant 7th chord indicated in Figure 97A has been changed into minor 7th chords with a flat 5. For example, in measure 3 to D-7(♭5), in measure 5 to D-7(♭5) and in measure 6 to E-7(♭5).

4. Realize the 6-note voicings utilized in measure 2, the A7(⁺¹¹♭9), in measure 4, the CM9(6), in measure 5, the G13(⁺¹¹♭9), and in measure 7, the G13(+11) are an extension of the "method".

5. Realize the 7-note voicings utilized in measure 8, the F9(13), in measure 9, the E♭13(+11), D7(♭9♭5) and in measure 10, D♭M9, CM9(+11), are an extension of the "method".

6. Realize the use of the augmented 11th in the major chord appears in measure 10, the CM9(+11).

Figure 97B

E. Utilizing the Substitute Chord on the Flatted Fifth

The following Figure 98A illustrates basic chords notated above the excerpted melody of the composition "All The Things You Are" to be harmonized. See Figure 98B for an illustration of harmonizing the following:

1. The dominant 7th chord on the flatted fifth as a substitute chord.

2. The minor 7th chord as a substitute chord. Also note the analysis precedes the figure.

Figure 98A

"ALL THE THINGS YOU ARE"

Medium Bright   By Jerome Kern & Oscar Hammerstein II

Analysis of a Harmonized Melody

Analysis of Figure 98B:

1. Realize that the basic notated chords, as given in Figure 98A, have been embellished within the rules of the method in Figure 98B.

2. Realize that a substitute chord is used in place of the E♭7 chord originally indicated in measure 3 of Figure 98A. For example: 1) the A7 chord, located on the flatted fifth of the E♭7 chord, is the substitute chord for the E♭7 and 2) the E-7 chord, located on the perfect fifth above the A7 chord, is the substitute chord for A7, which then resolves to the A7 chord for which it was substituted.

3. Realize the use of "specific voicings" when the major 7th is the melody note. See measure 4.

Figure 98B

Medium Bright

- 119 -

F. Altering the Diminished 7th Chord into a Dominant 7th Chord

Realize that by altering a diminished 7th chord into a dominant 7th chord, the dominant 7th chord can be used as a substitute chord for the diminished 7th chord. Realize that there are four dominant 7th chords that are possible substitute chords for each diminished 7th chord. To determine the dominant 7th chords that can be used as substitute chords for the diminished 7th chord, a simple solution is to lower each of the four notes of the diminished 7th chord one-half step and construct a dominant 7th chord upon each of those notes. However, realize the reason for this is that as each tone of the diminished 7th chord is lowered by one-half step, a dominant 7th chord is produced. For example, Figure 99 Example 1 illustrates the basic C°7 chord; realize that by lowering the root of the chord, for example the C, by one-half step to B, the chord is now a B7. Example 2 illustrates the 3rd of the chord, the E♭, lowered by one-half step to D; the chord is now D7. Example 3 illustrates the diminished 5th of the chord, the G♭, lowered by one-half step to F; the chord is now an F7. Example 4 illustrates the diminished 7th of the chord, the A, lowered by one-half step, to A♭; the chord is now an A♭7. Realize that each dominant 7th chord has three notes in common with the diminished 7th chord.

Figure 99

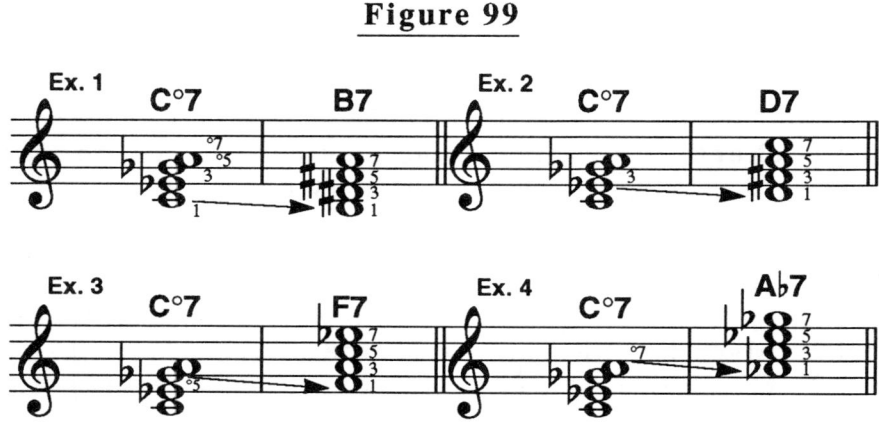

G. Choosing the Appropriate Dominant 7th Chord as a Substitute Chord for the Diminished 7th Chord

Now that the player knows how to alter the diminished 7th chord into dominant 7th chords to be used as possible substitute chords for the diminished 7th chord, the player needs to realize the following:

1. When to use the substitute dominant 7th chord for the diminished 7th chord.

2. How to choose the appropriate dominant 7th chord as the substitute chord for the diminished 7th chord.

At this time the player needs to realize that in choosing the appropriate dominant 7th chord, as the substitute chord for the diminished 7th chord, it is not automatic, for at times, a dominant 7th chord may not be appropriate and therefore the diminished 7th chord must be used. However, when it is possible to use a substitute chord for the diminished 7th chord, the following two approaches can help the player to determine the appropriate substitute chord.

Approach #1

Know the chord that follows the Diminished 7th chord and refer to the **root** of that chord, as a **tonic (I) chord**. This tonic (I) chord can be Major (I), Minor (I-), Minor 7 (I-7) or a Dominant 7th (I7) chord. Then choose from among the possible substitute dominant 7th chords (V7), the dominant 7th chord that would normally resolve to that **root of the chord**, in the progression of V7 to I. To illustrate this approach, the following Figure 100 Example 1, contains a G♯°7 chord followed by the A-7 chord. Realize the possible substitute chords for the G♯°7 chord (that which evolves by lowering each note of the diminished 7th chord one-half step) are G7, B♭7, D♭7, and E7. However, in selecting the appropriate substitute chord for the G♯°7, we have chosen the E7 chord, as illustrated in Example 2 because the E7 chord resolves to the A-7 chord in the progression of V7 to I-7.

Approach #2

As stated in approach #1, refer to the chord that follows the diminished 7th chord as a **tonic (I) chord**. Then choose the dominant 7th chord (V7) that resolves to that tonic (I) chord. However, when there is no dominant 7th chord that can resolve to that tonic chord in the progression of V7 to I, choose the dominant 7th chord that would resolve to that **root of the chord**, in the progression of VII7 to I. To illustrate this approach, the following Figure 101 Example 1 contains a B♭°7 followed by the G Major chord. Realize the possible substitute chords for the B♭°7 chord (that which evolves by lowering each note of the diminished 7th chord one-half step) are A7, C7, E♭7 and F♯7. However, in selecting the appropriate substitute chord for the B♭°7 we have chosen the F♯7 chord, as illustrated in example 2, because the F♯7 chord resolves to the G Major chord in the progression of VII7 to I.

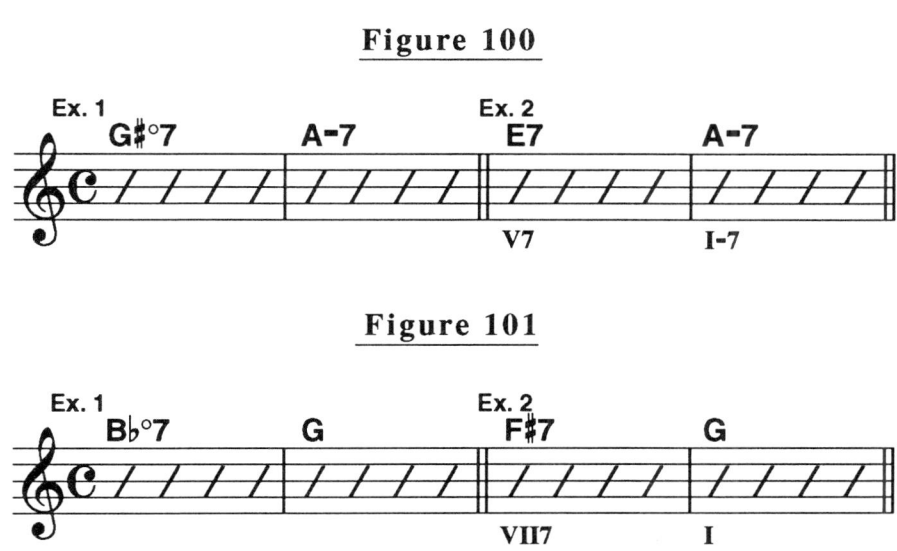

Figure 100

Figure 101

- 121 -

H. Utilizing Substitute Chords for Diminished 7th Chords and Dominant 7th Chords; Interpretation of the Minor 6th Chord When Preceding a Dominant 7th Chord

The following Figure 102A illustrates basic chords notated above the excerpted melody of the composition "But Beautiful" to be harmonized. See Figure 102B for an illustration of harmonizing the melody utilizing the following:

1. Substitute chords for the Diminished 7th and Dominant 7th chords.

2. Interpretation of the Minor 6th chord when preceding a Dominant 7th chord. Also note the analysis precedes the figure.

Figure 102A

"BUT BEAUTIFUL"   By James VanHeusen &
Slowly with expression   Johnny Burke

Analysis of a Harmonized Melody

Analysis of Figure 102B:

1. Realize that the basic notated chords, as given in Figure 102A, have been embellished within the rules of the method in Figure 102B.

2. Realize that dominant 7th chords are used as substitute chords for the diminished 7th chords, originally indicated in measure 2 and 4 of Figure 102A. Also realize that minor 7th chords are used as substitute chords for these dominant 7th chords. For example: 1) in measure 2 the E7 chord is the substitute chord for the G#°7 chord. Realize that approach #1, as explained on page 121, was used in choosing the appropriate substitute chord. Also realize the B-7(♭5) chord is the substitute chord for the E7 chord; 2) in measure 4 the F#7 chord is the substitute chord for the B♭°7 chord. Realize that approach #2, as explained on page 121, was used in choosing the appropriate substitute chord. Notice each substitute chord resolves to the dominant 7th chord for which it was substituted. For example, the B-7(♭5) to E7($^{13}_{♭9}$) and C#-7(♭5) to F#7($^{13}_{♭9}$).

3. Realize that in measure 6, the D-6 chord preceding the dominant 7th chord indicated in Figure 102A has been changed into a B minor 7th chord with a flat 5.

4. Realize that a minor 7th chord is used as a substitute chord for the dominant 7th chord originally indicated in measures 7 and 8 of Figure 102A. For example, in measures 7 and 8 the E-7 chord is the substitute chord for the A7 chord. Realize the E-7 chord resolves to the A7 chord, the chord for which it was substituted in each measure. Also realize that when a dominant 7th chord is indicated for two measures, there are various ways in which the substitute minor 7th chord and the dominant 7th chord can be broken down as previously illustrated in Figure 93 on page 115.

Figure 102B

Slowly with expression

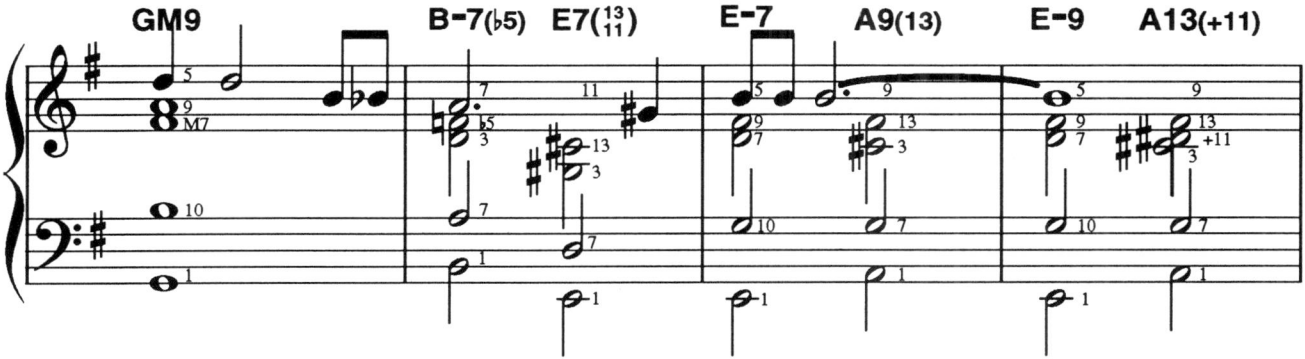

I. Interpretation of the Notated Chords Contained in Sheet Music and in the Fakebooks

When notated chords are indicated in sheet music, such as a basic chord (for example C Maj.) or a specific chord (for example C6(9), realize that these chords often signify the content of the chords used in the arrangement in the sheet music. Also, realize that the notated chords indicated in the fakebooks reflect those notated chords in sheet music. Therefore, when interpreting the notated chords indicated in both the sheet music and in the fakebooks, realize that the player is not restricted to using the content of the basic and/or the specific notated chords indicated. However, the player should interpret those chords as a suggestion and then exercise his ability to embellish both the basic and specific notated chords as outlined in the "method."

At times an augmented chord appears in notation. For example, "C augmented" (notated C+) contains C, E and G♯. This type of chord is always a three note chord and, although these notes may be doubled, the results are not to be confused with the 5-note harmony offered in this text. Instead the results will be traditional harmony; for example, the basic triad and the doubling of those tones freely. Of course, it is important to realize that at times traditional rather than modern harmony is desirable, as in cases where the melody line and character of the music dictate the use of such traditional harmony. When this occurs, it is the player's responsibility to recognize when it is appropriate to use traditional harmony and when to use modern harmony; on the basis of his musical experience, he will make the necessary adjustments.

CLOSING SUMMARY

The material presented throughout each of the chapters contained in this text brings together tenets of basic theory that are conventionally left isolated into a total system of harmony that we have called the "Amadiean Creed."

By applying the "method" to each of the specific types of chords that are found in popular music, standards and jazz, we have illustrated that 5-note, and at times, 4-note chord voicings are complete within themselves and thus form a foundation for modern harmony upon which the "method" can be expanded to 6-note and 7-note chord voicings.

Also, realize that this text does note presume to be the "last word" in establishing a practice for modern harmony. On the contrary, it is the beginning.

Therefore, it is suggested to the player that the method serve as a basis for a harmonic practice that effectively guides a player to creatively construct chord voicings and harmonize a melody in the modern vein, one which he can continue to develop and expand.

APPENDIX I CHORD VOICINGS

The purpose of the Appendix is to illustrate the application of the method for voicing each of the notated chords given in the Assignment contained in Letter I, Exercise I and II of each chapter and thus afford the player an opportunity to compare and evaluate his application of the method. In addition, the player must realize that the voicings he chooses reflect his taste and his ability to create within the method; and therefore, his voicings need note be the same as those contained in the appendix, for there are numerous possibilities of voicing each of the notated chords. However, the content of his voicings must be the same. Also, play each chord voicing in other registers and evaluate the sound. This applies to all exercises in this Appendix.

Chapter I: Exercise I

"AMADIEAN CREED"

Step 1
(2 notes)

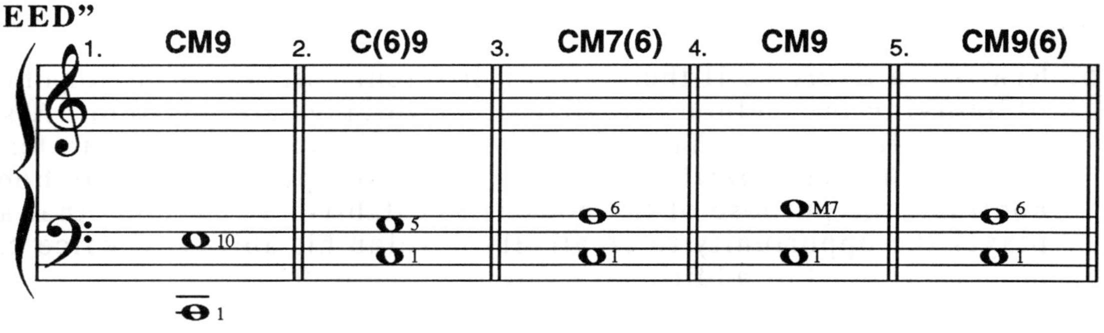

Step 2
(add 1 note)

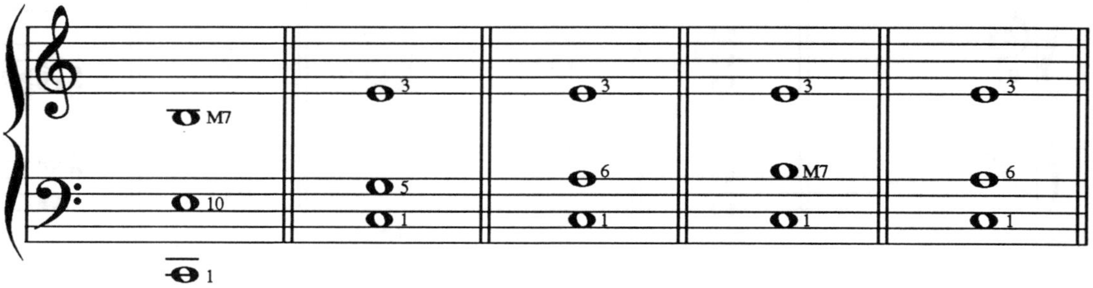

Step 3
(add 2 notes)

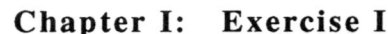

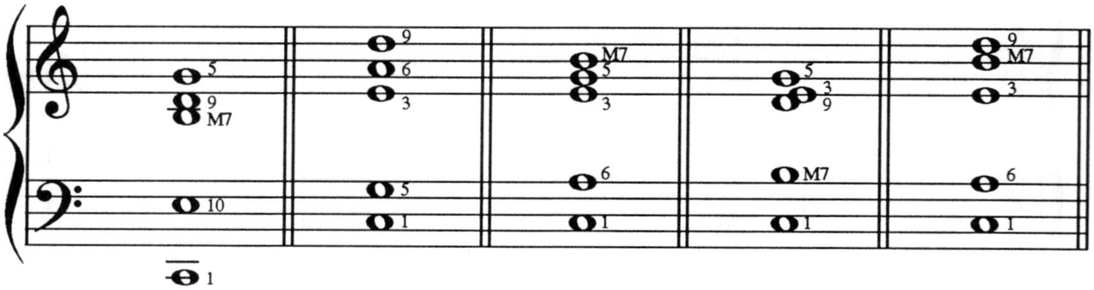

Step 4
(Notation)

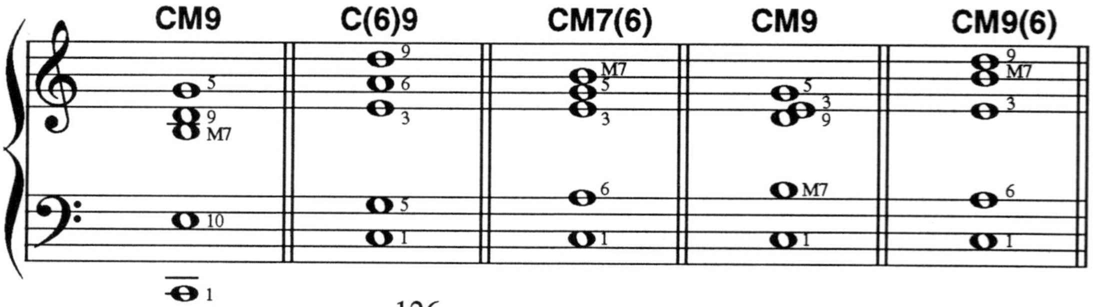

APPENDIX I CHORD VOICINGS

Chapter I: Exercise II

1. Realize measures 1, 5, 9 and 13 are Major 9th chords. Notice each voicing is different.

2. Realize measures 2, 6, 10 and 14 are Major 6(9) chords. Notice each voicing is different.

3. Realize measures 3, 7 and 11 are Major 9(6) chords. Notice each voicing is different.

4. Realize measures 4, 8 and 12 are Major 7(6) chords. Notice each chord voicing is different.

5. Realize in Exercise II there are 14 different voicings of major chords as a result of applying the method. Realize other voicings are possible. Also, the player need not feel that he has to memorize each voicing in order to learn them. **Realize that memorizing voicings is not the purpose of this book.** On the contrary, the purpose of the book is to establish a "method" that affords the player the opportunity to creatively develop his ability to voice chords in the modern vein. For additional exercises, see p. 9.

APPENDIX I   CHORD VOICINGS

Chapter II: Exercise I

"AMADIEAN CREED"

Step 1
(2 notes)

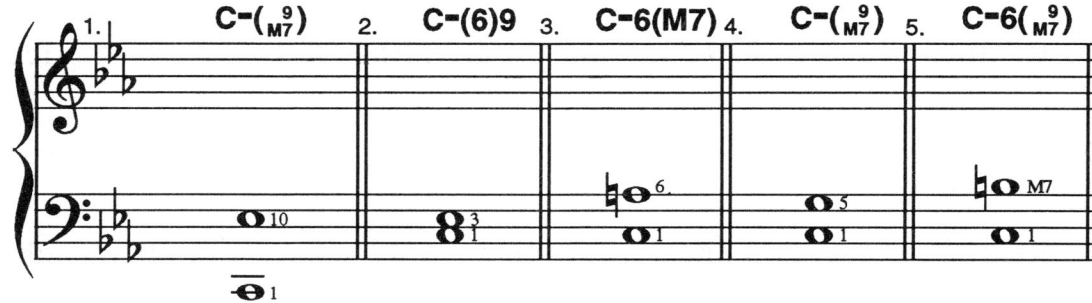

Step 2
(add 1 note)

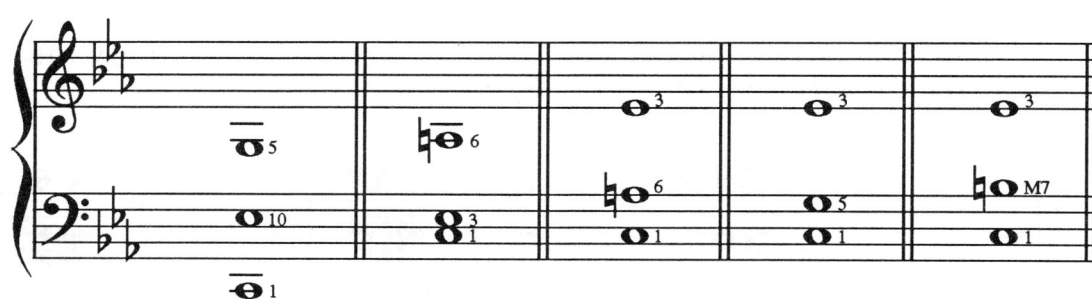

Step 3
(add 2 notes)

Step 4
(Notation)

APPENDIX I   CHORD VOICINGS

Chapter II: Exercise II

1. Realize measures 1, 5, 10 and 13 are Minor $\left(^9_{M7}\right)$ chords. Notice each voicing is different.

2. Realize measures 2, 7, 8, 9 and 14 are Minor 6(9) chords. Notice each voicing is different.

3. Realize measures 3, 6 and 11 are Minor $6\left(^9_{M7}\right)$ chords. Notice each voicing is different.

4. Realize measures 4 and 12 are Minor 6(M7) chords. Notice each chord voicing is different.

5. Realize in Exercise II there are 14 different voicings of minor chords as a result of applying the method. Realize other voicings are possible; therefore, to develop a creative approach for voicing minor chords, apply the "method". For additional exercises, see page 28.

Chapter III: Exercise I

"AMADIEAN CREED"

Step 1
(2 notes)

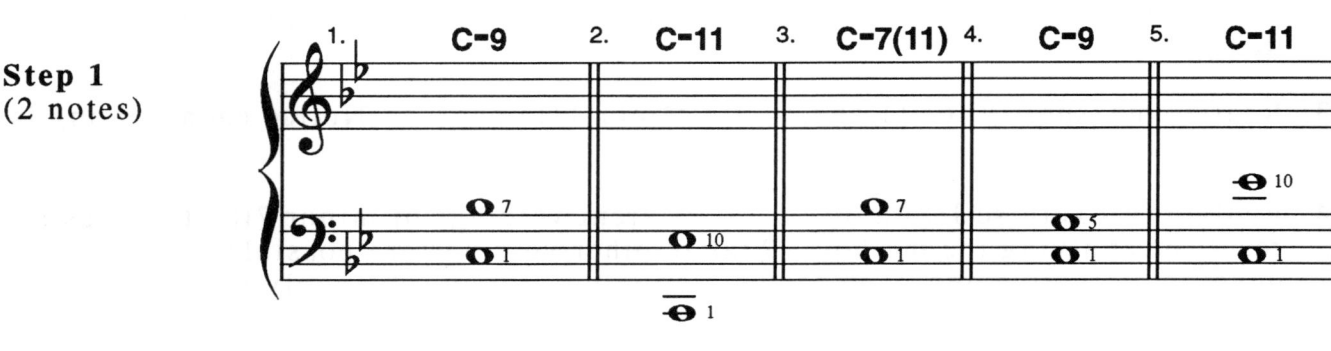

Step 2
(add 1 note)

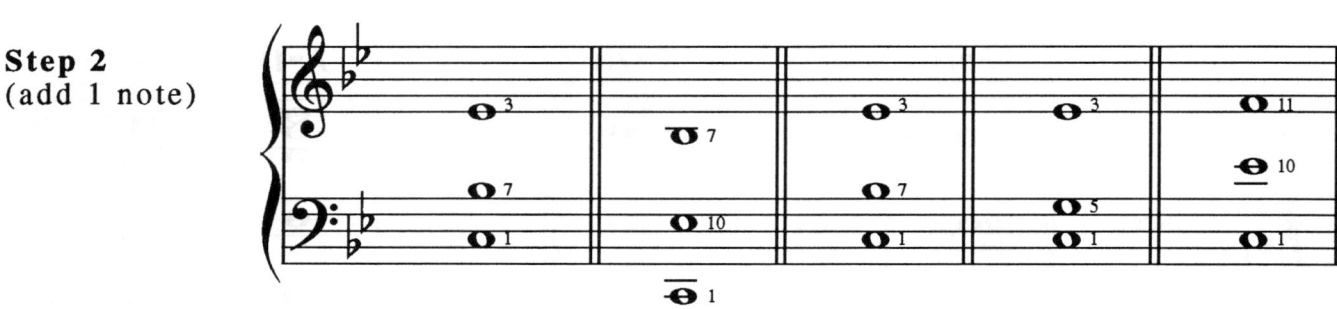

Step 3
(add 2 notes)

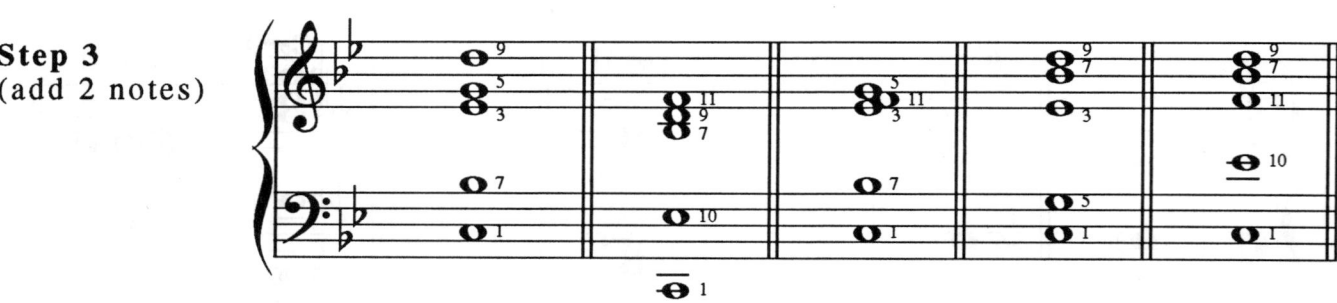

Step 4
(Notation)

APPENDIX I CHORD VOICINGS

Chapter III: Exercise II

1. Realize measures 1, 5, 8, 9, 12 and 13 are Minor 9th chords. Notice each voicing is different.

2. Realize measures 2, 4, 7 and 10 are Minor 7(11) chords. Notice each voicing is different.

3. Realize measures 3, 6, 11 and 14 are Minor 11th chords. Notice each voicing is different.

4. Realize in Exercise II, there are 14 different voicings of minor 7th chords as a result of applying the method. Realize other voicings are possible; therefore, to develop a creative approach for voicing minor 7th chords, apply the "method". For additional exercises, see page 46.

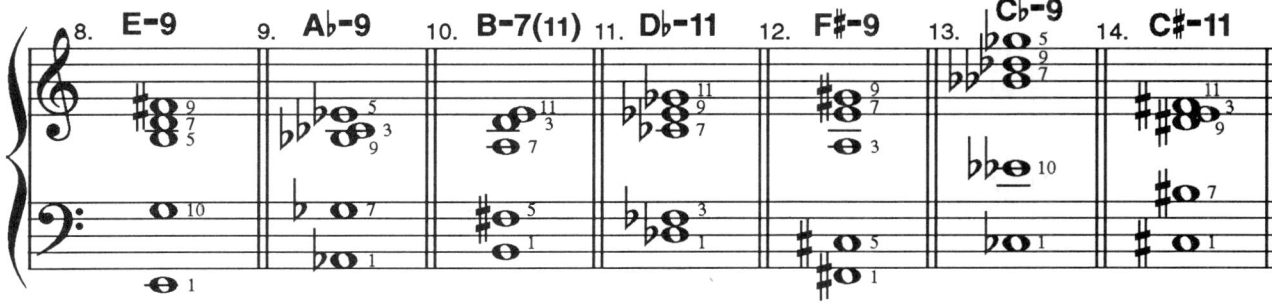

APPENDIX I   CHORD VOICINGS

Chapter IV: Exercise I

"AMADIEAN CREED"

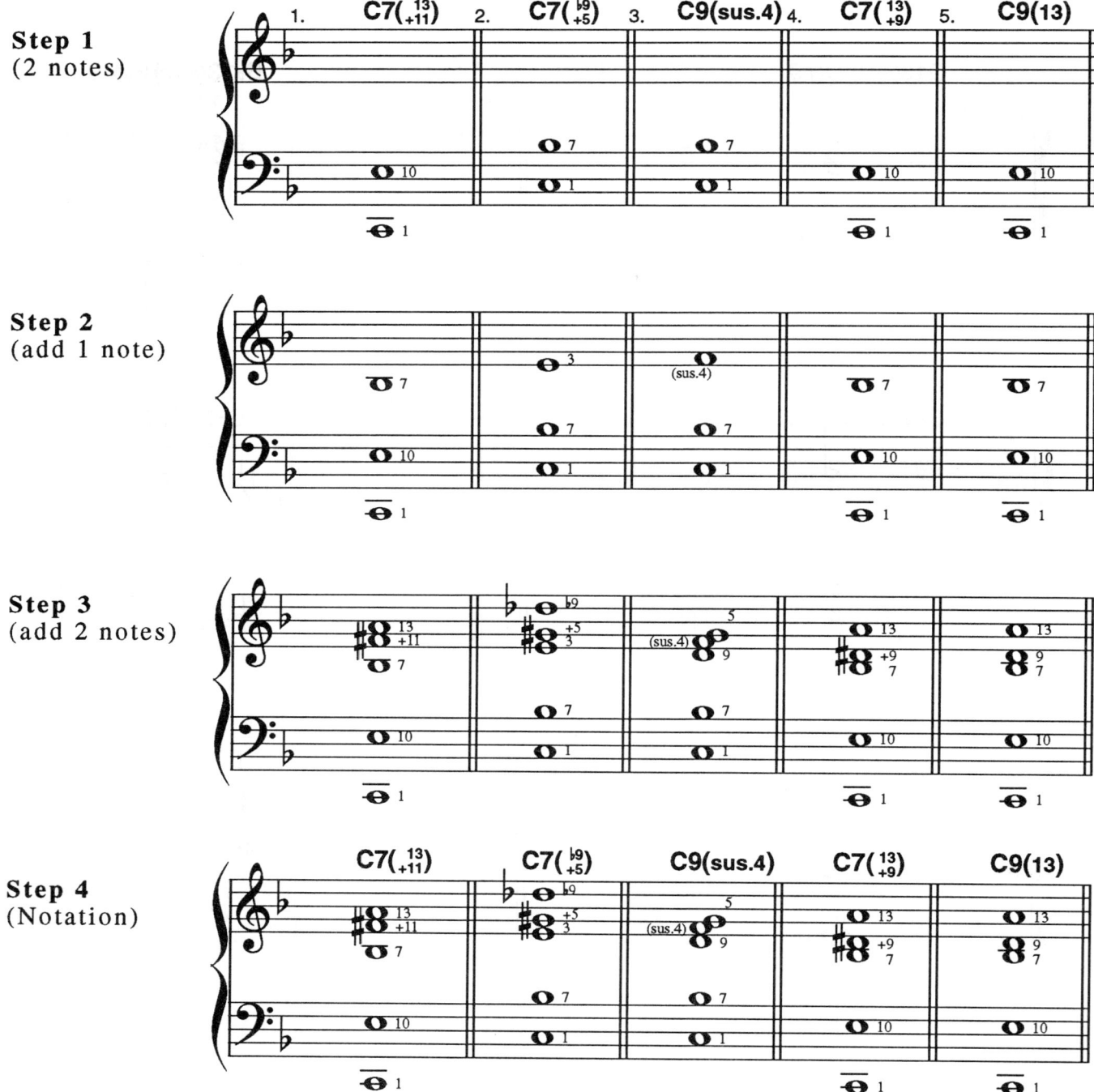

Chapter IV: Exercise II

1. Realize in Exercise II, there are 12 different voicings of dominant 7th chords as a result of applying the method. Notice the resolution of the dominant 7th chord to the major chord completes a musical idea.

2. Realize other voicings are possible; therefore, to develop a creative approach for voicing dominant 7th chords, apply the method. For additional writing exercises, see p. 69.

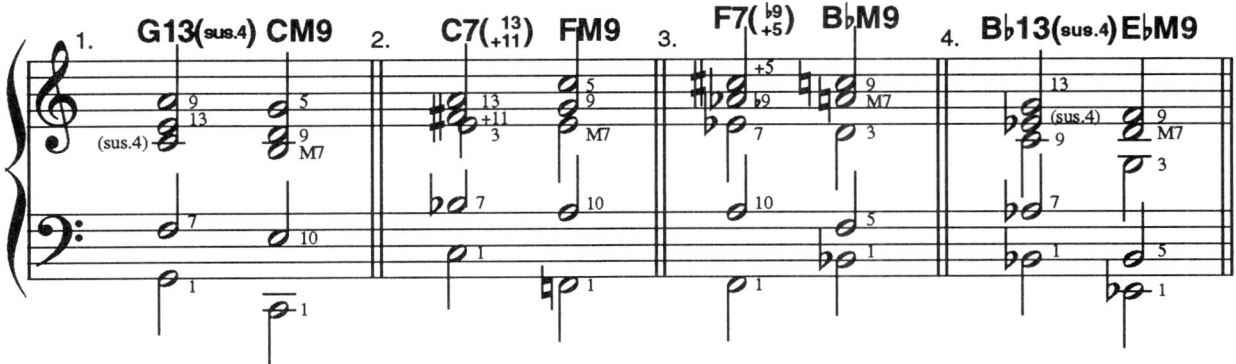

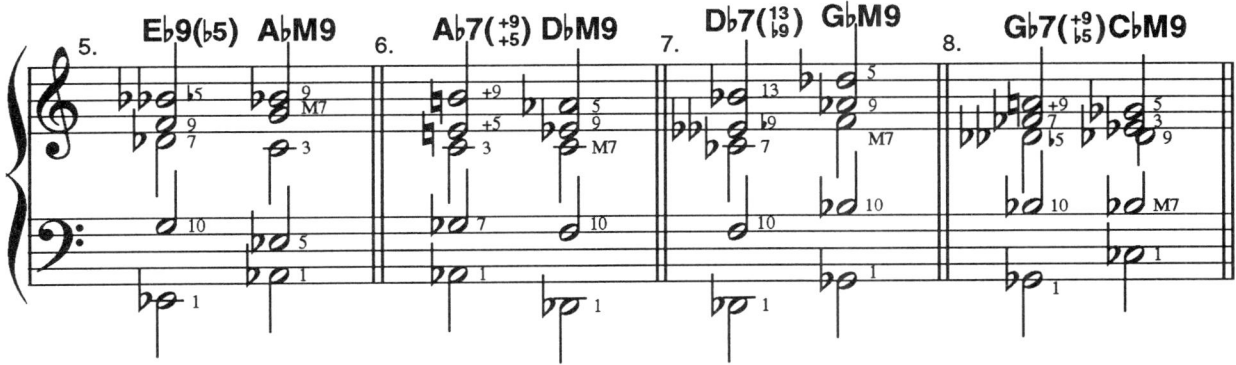

Chapter V: Exercise I

"AMADIEAN CREED"

Step 1
(2 notes)

Step 2
(add 1 note)

Step 3
(add 2 notes)

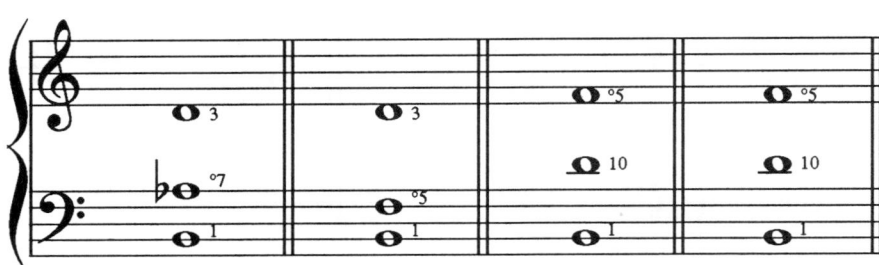

Step 4
(Notation)

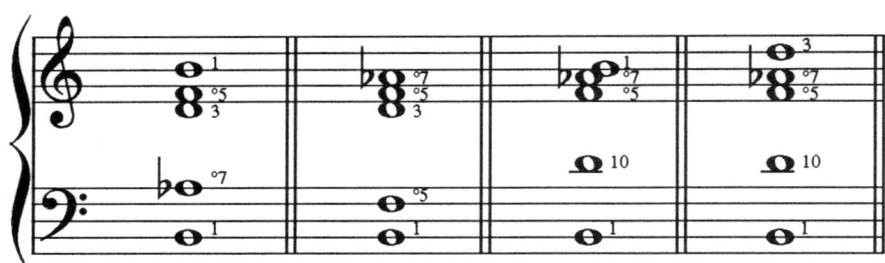

APPENDIX I CHORDS VOICINGS

Chapter V: Exercise II

1. Realize measures 1 through 8 are Diminished 7th chords. Notice each voicing is different.

2. Realize for simplicity the double flat is avoided when indicating the diminished 7th of the chord in measures 1, 3 and 6.

3. Realize in Exercise II there are 8 different voicings of diminished 7th chords as a result of applying the method. The diminished 7th chord is unique in its harmonic limitations because of the restricted number of notes from which to choose. For additonal writing exercises, see p. 95.

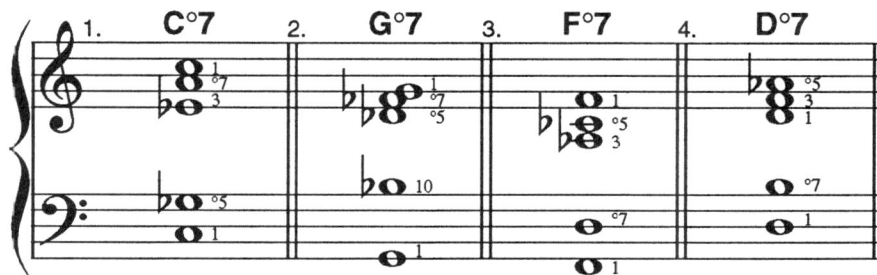

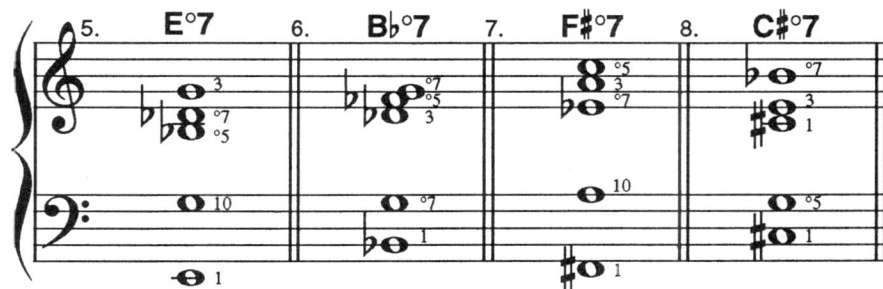

APPENDIX II   HARMONIZED MELODIES

The purpose of the Appendix is to illustrate the application of the method when harmonizing a melody and thus afford the player the opportunity to compare and evaluate his application of the method. In addition, the player must realize that the embellishment and voicings that he chooses reflect his taste and his ability to create within the method and therefore his choice of embellished tones and voicings need not be the same as those contained in the appendix. However, by comparing the examples below with the player's own harmonization, he should arrive at a better sense of his own potential and how the method is helping him to develop it.

CHAPTER I: Exercises 1 through 5

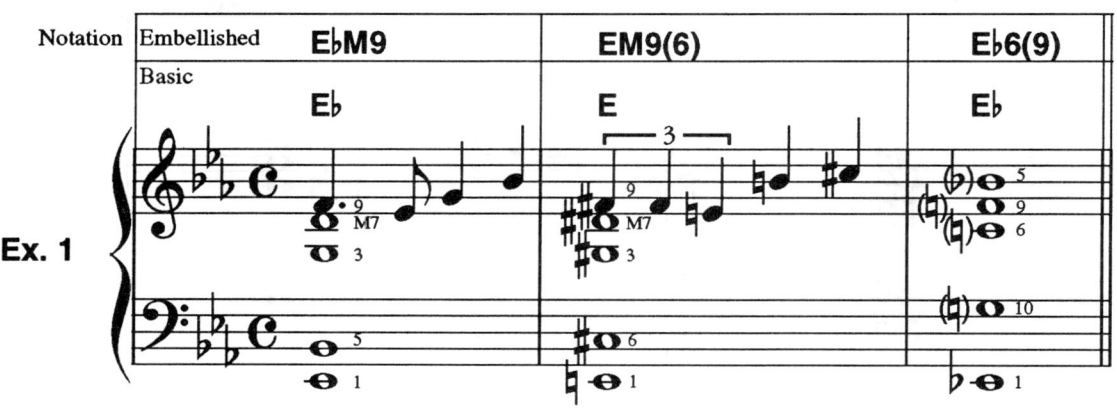

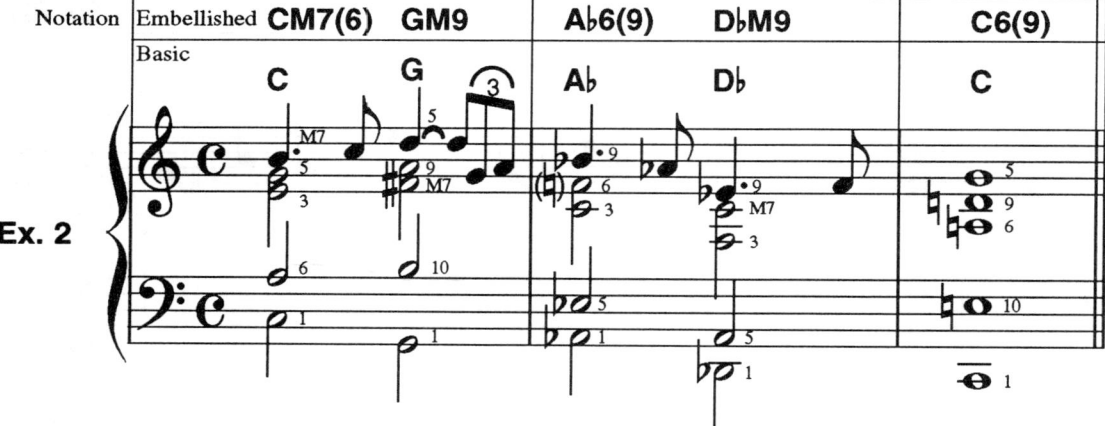

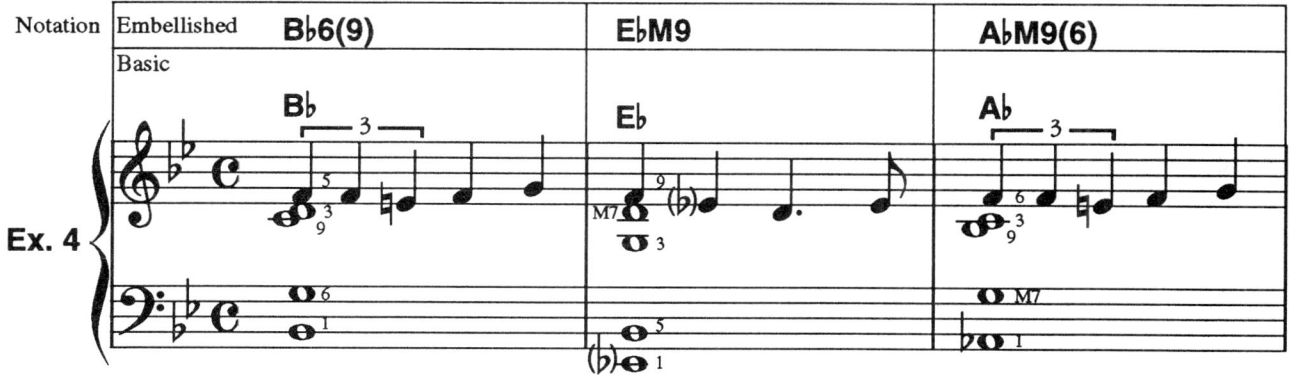

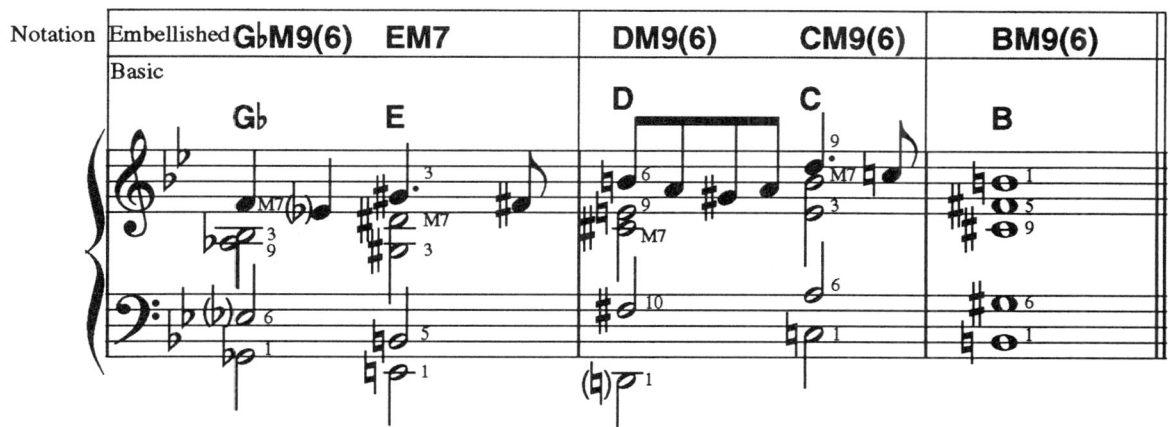

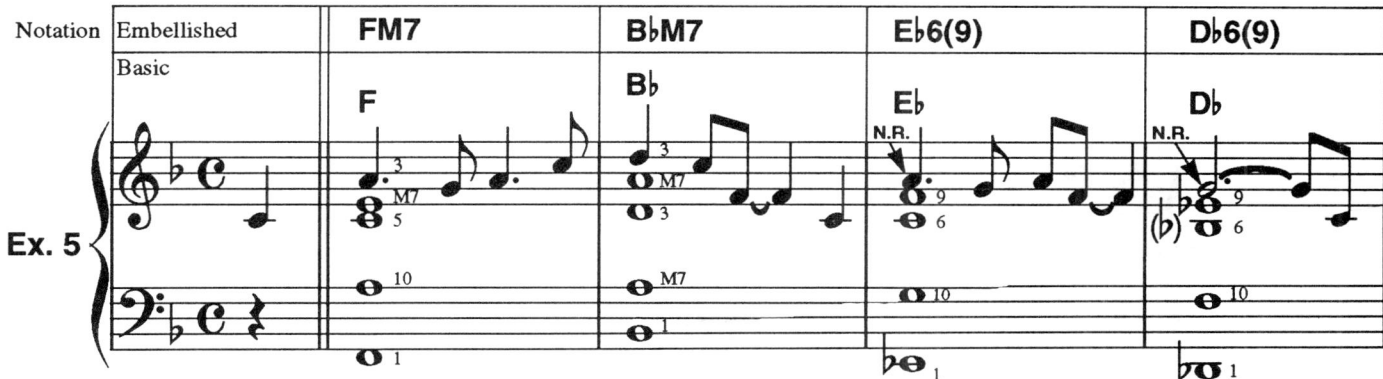

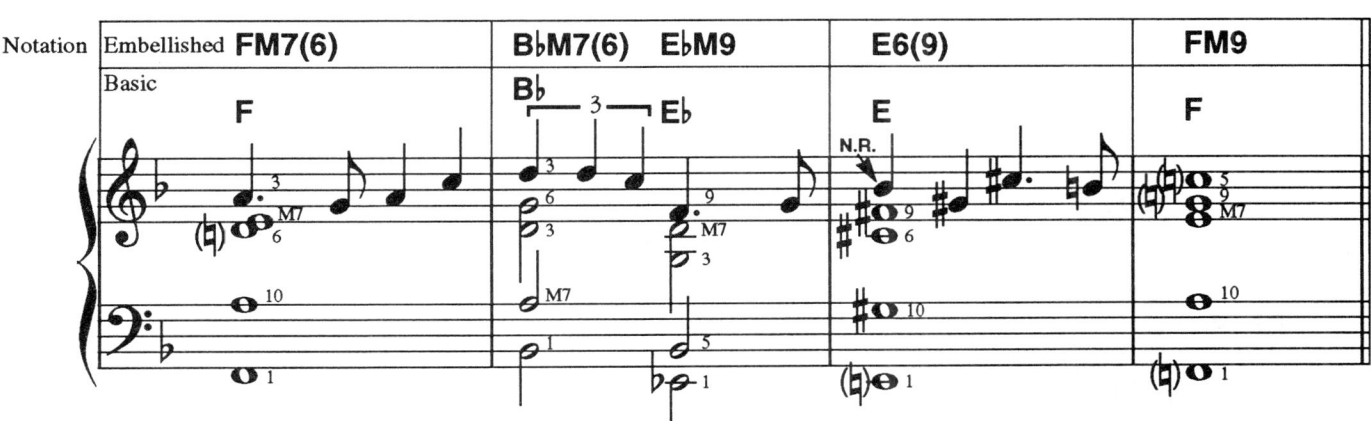

CHAPTER II: Exercises 1 through 5

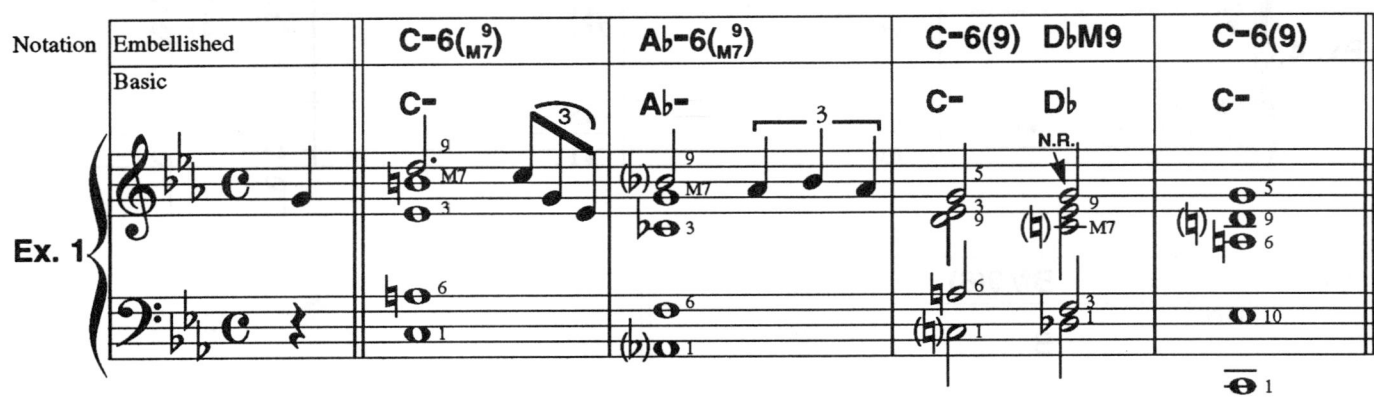

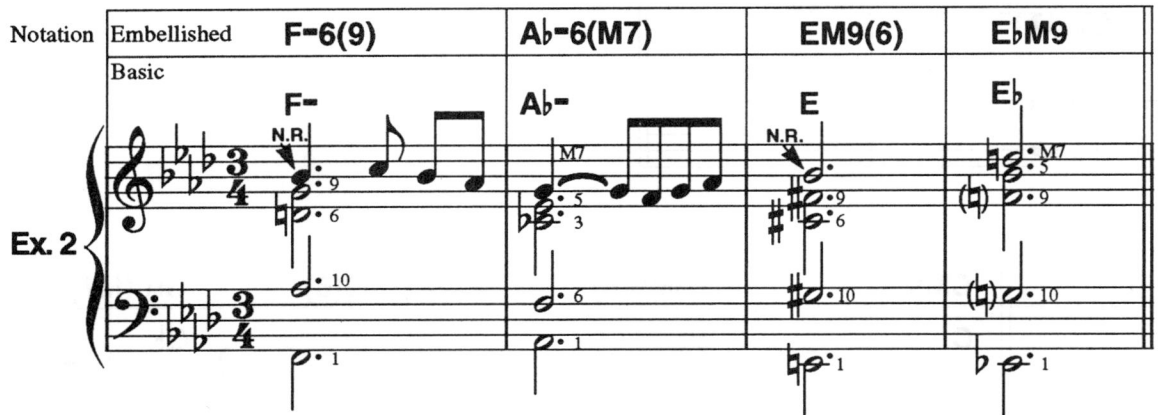

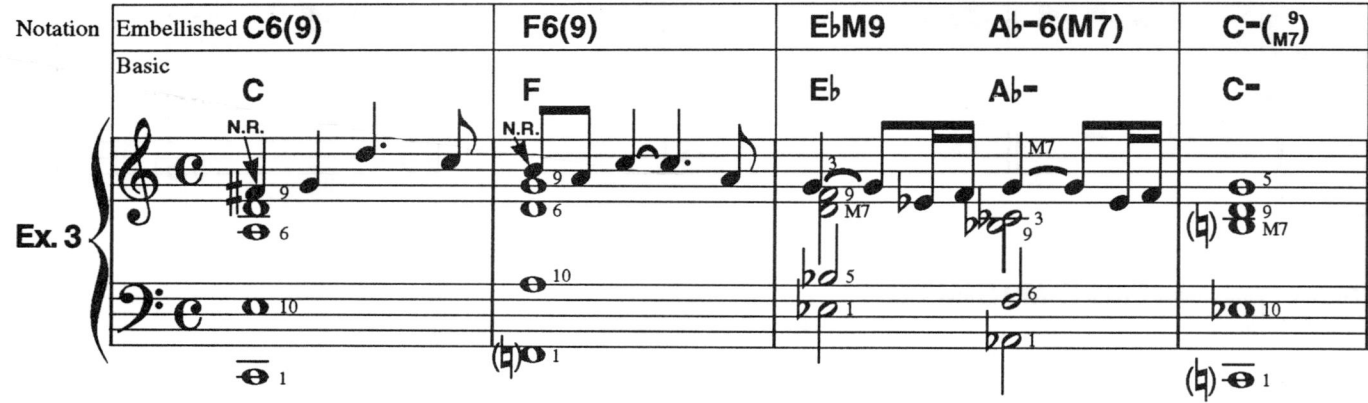

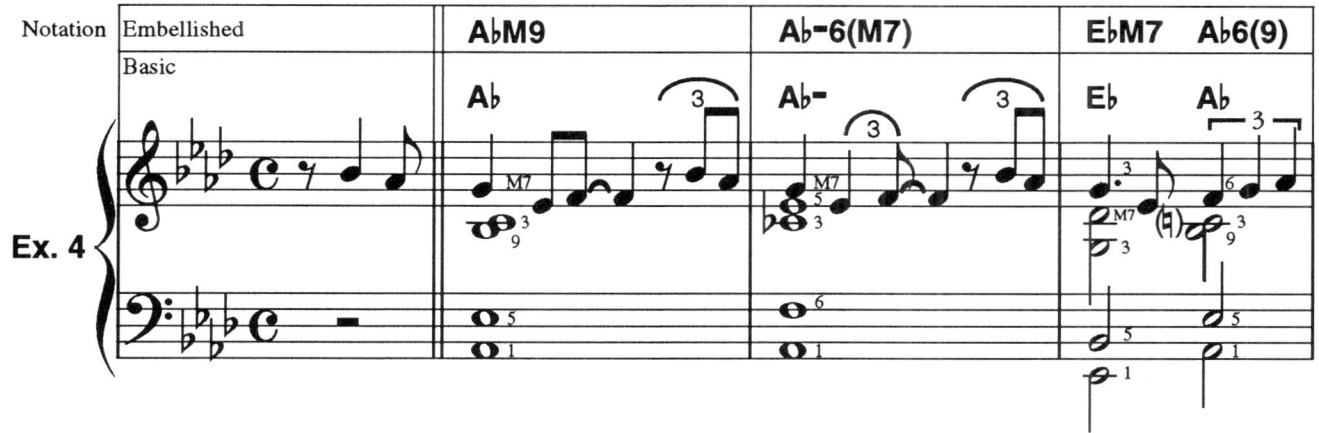

Ex. 4

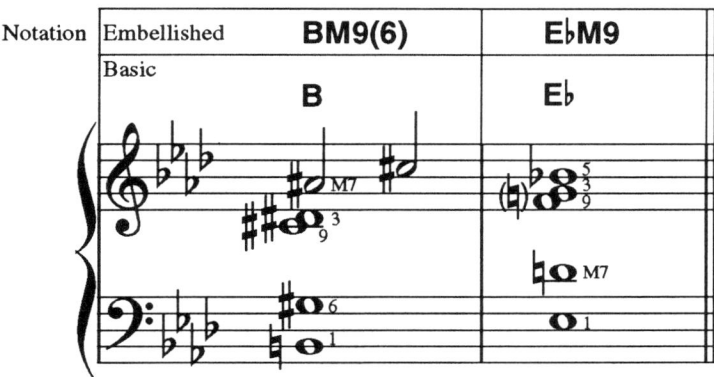

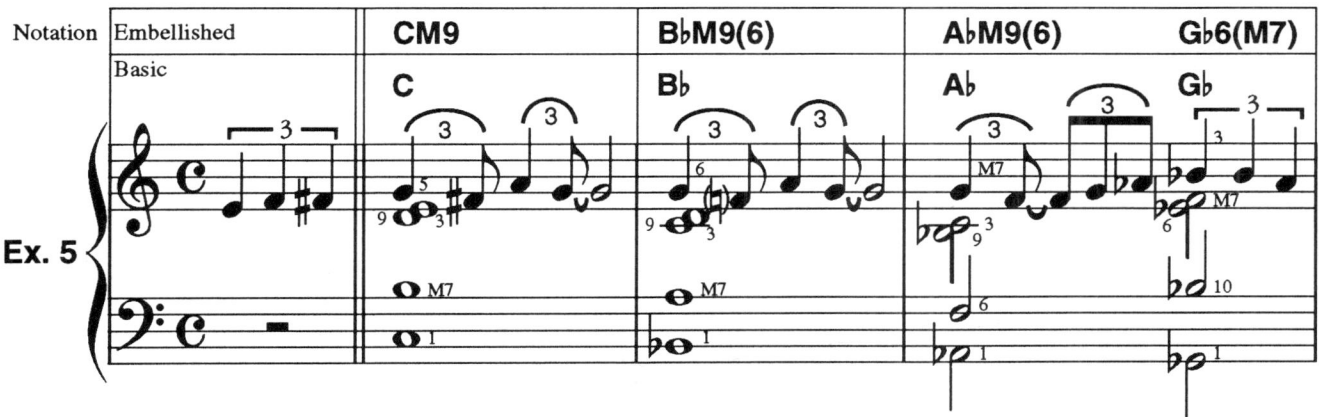

Ex. 5

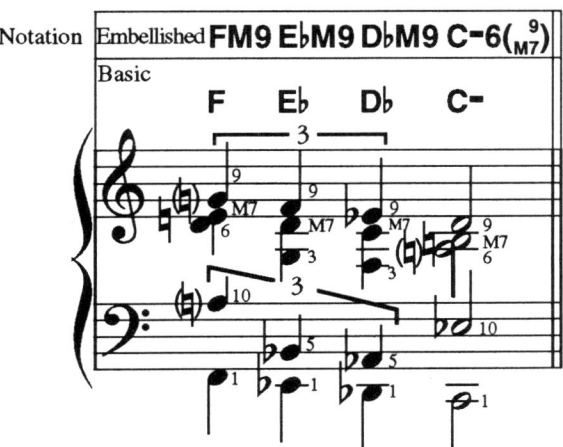

CHAPTER III: Exercises 1 through 5

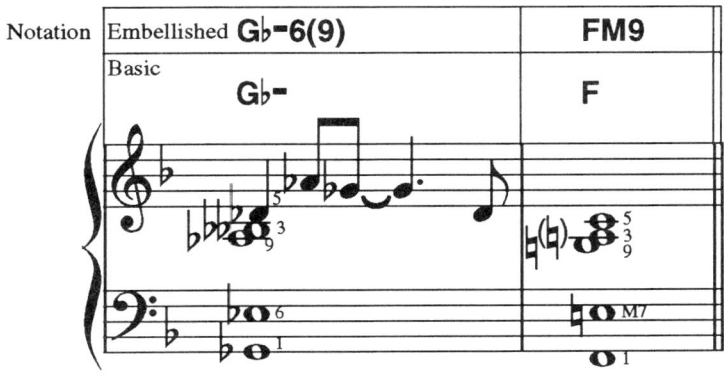

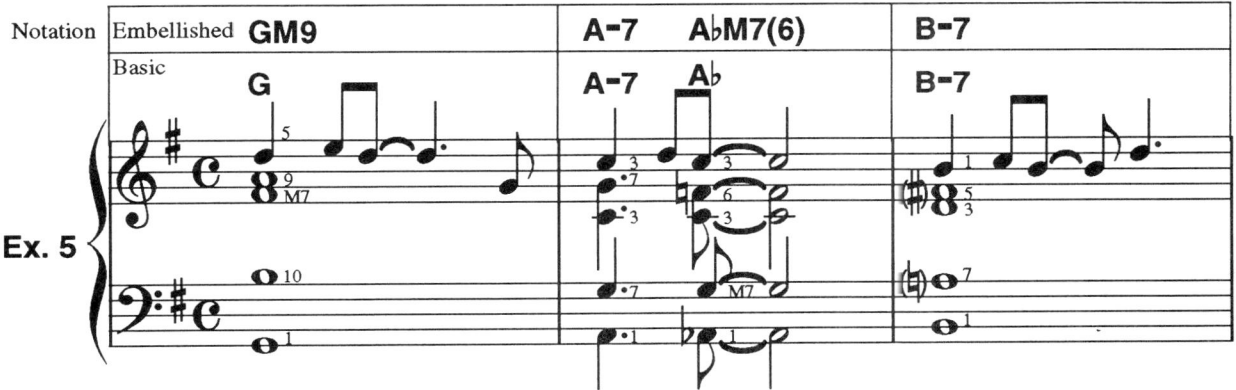

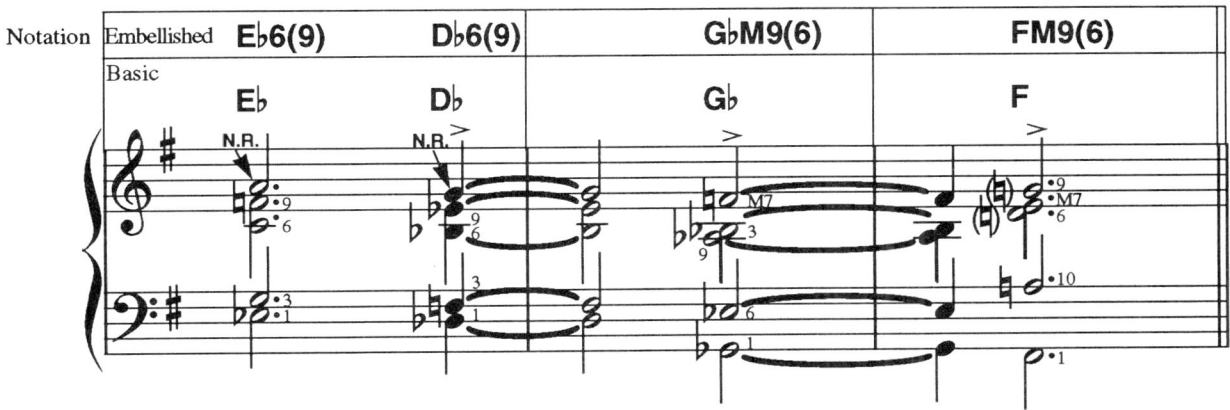

Slowly with a beat

"ALONE WITH YOU"

By Jimmy Amadie

Ex. 1

Medium Up   "TUNE UP"   By Miles Davis

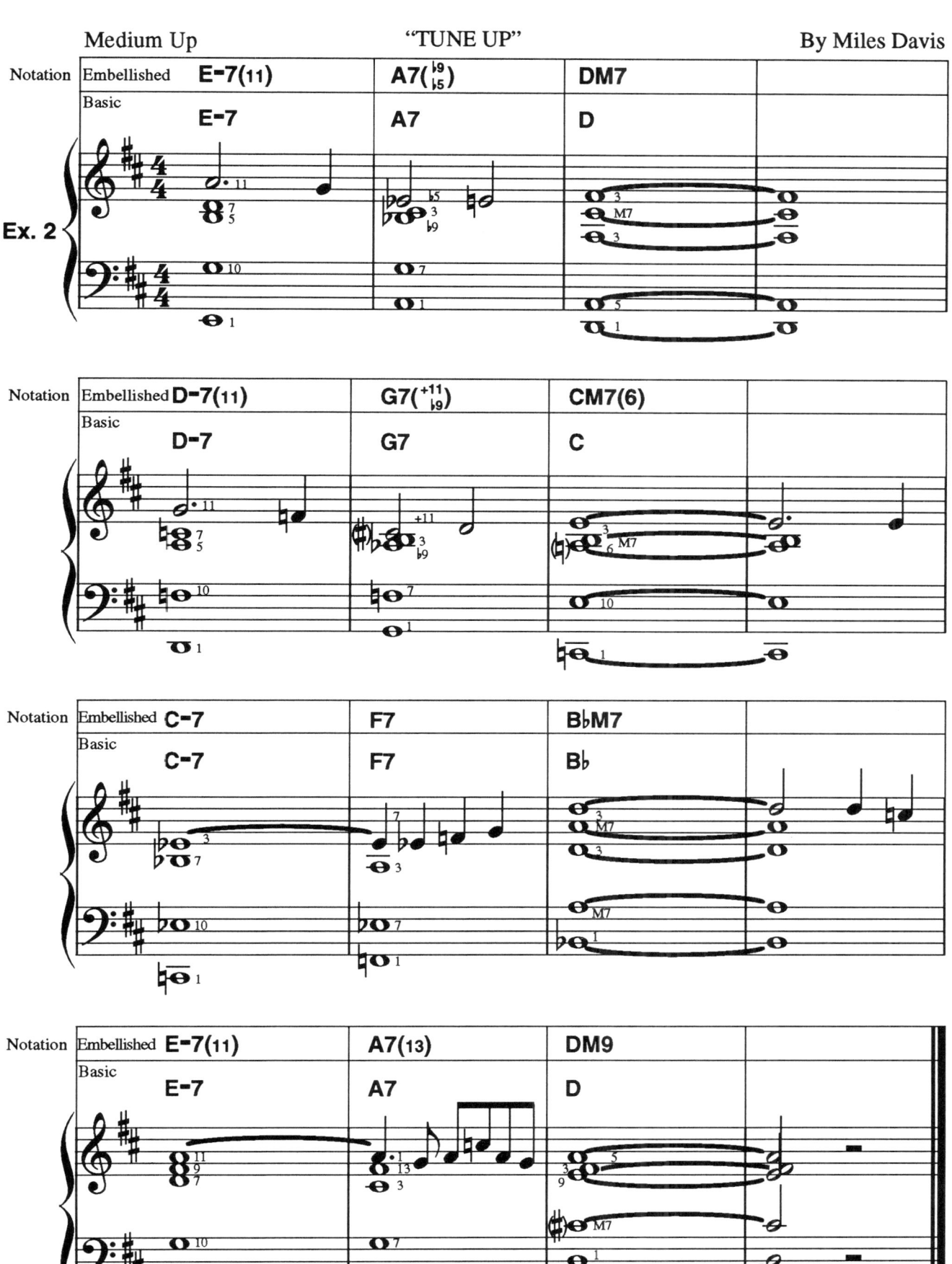

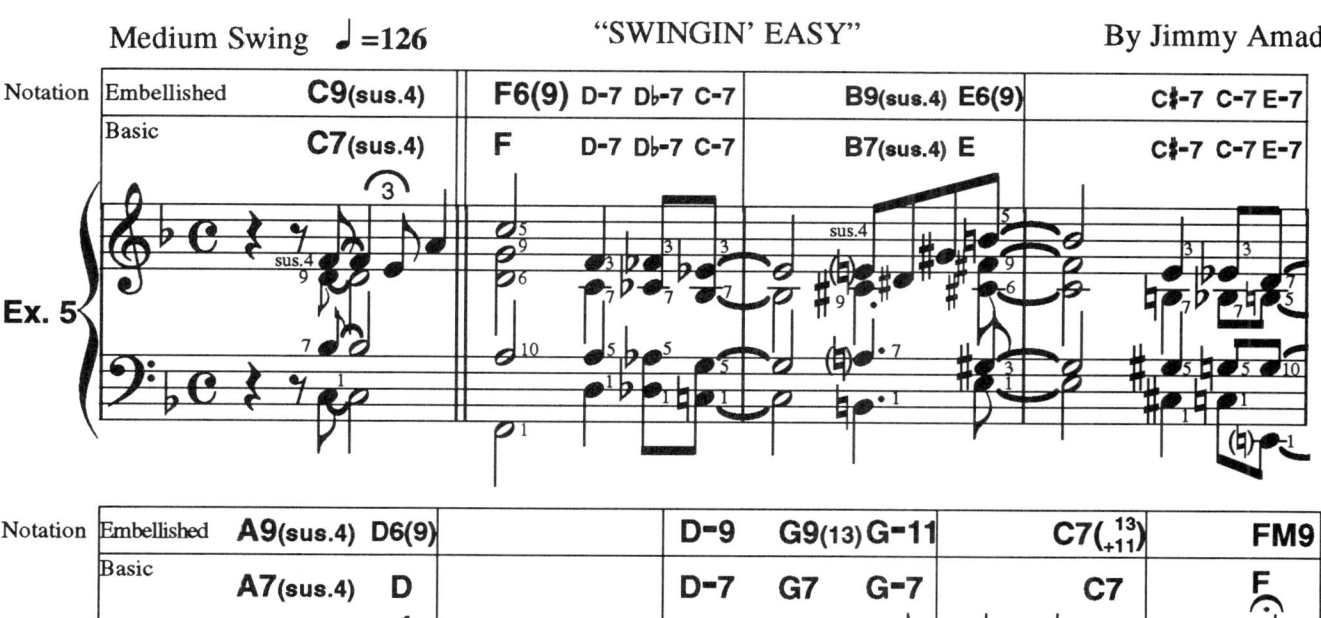

CHAPTER V
Composition 1
"YOU'RE THE ONE FOR ME"

By Jimmy Amadie

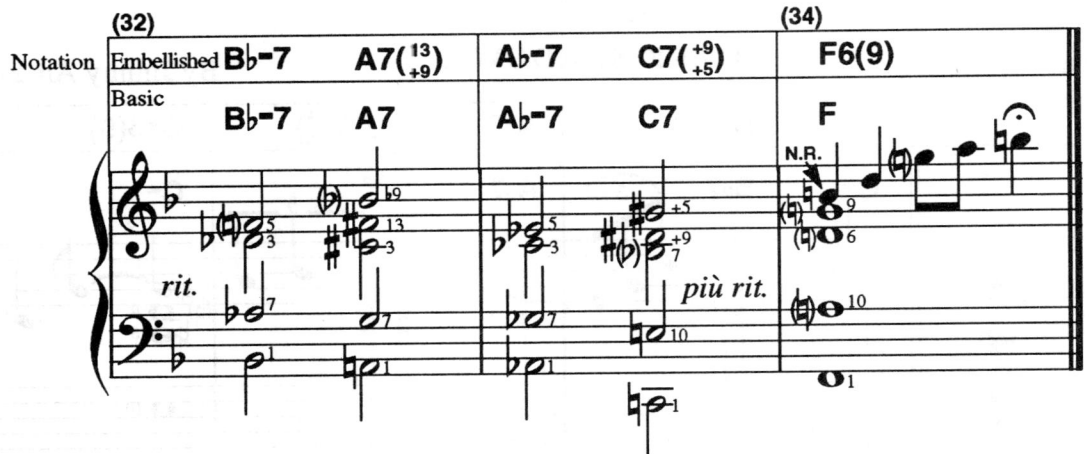

Composition 2

"DARK SHADOW"

By Jimmy Amadie